Praise for
NEW STEP

"Abby bares all about her journey into entrepreneurship. It's a funny, raw and real look at what happens—both professionally and personally—when you follow your intuition. I am so grateful for her willingness to write the truth and share her vulnerability about the journey of an entrepreneur . . . because it's a JOURNEY! Her story is a gift, and it makes you believe anything is possible."

MELANIE HELLWIG WHITE, CEO, Hellwig Products Co.

"Follow a woman as she steps into her calling. Abby's success stemmed from having the guts to ask a single question no one had thought to ask before. But she made sure to have the heartfelt dedication to follow it through. This story is a must read!"

ALI BROWN, Founder + CEO, The Trust

"I finished this book in two days—all while laughing and crying. It's such an inspiring, motivating, and empowering story that it will make you reevaluate your life and your business . . . it's impossible not to take action after you've read it. I know I did! Thank you from the bottom of my heart for sharing your story, Abby."

HELENA ESCALANTE, Entrepreneur-in-Residence, The New York Public Library

"As a business coach, I appreciate Abby's transparency. Too many times we get to see the 'cherry on top' version of an entrepreneur's success. But Abby candidly details her highs and lows coupled with the real-world hurdles of surpassing her wildest dreams. A must-read for anyone who feels their vision is bigger than their current state of being."

REBEKAH HALL, President, Kala

**THE MAKING OF AN ENTREPRENEUR AND HER
MULTI-MILLION DOLLAR COMPANY**

ABBY LOU WALKER

PRESIDENT AND CEO OF vivian lou

Copyright © 2023 Abby Lou Walker

All rights reserved. No part of this publication may be reproduced, distributed, or transmitted in any form or by any means, including photocopying, recording, or other electronic or mechanical methods, without the prior written permission of the publisher, except in the case of brief quotations embodied in reviews and certain other noncommercial uses permitted by copyright law.

Published by
MANDALA TREE PRESS
mandalatreepress.com

Paperback ISBN: 9781954801622
Hardcover with Dust Jacket ISBN: 9781954801646
Case Laminate Hardcover ISBN: 9781954801639
eBook ISBN: 9781954801653

BIO026000 BIOGRAPHY & AUTOBIOGRAPHY / Personal Memoirs
SEL027000 SELF-HELP / Personal Growth / Success
FAM054000 FAMILY & RELATIONSHIPS / Life Stages / Mid-Life

Cover design and typesetting by Kaitlin Barwick

vivianlou.com

TO THOSE WHO ARE MEANT FOR MORE,
HERE'S TO COURAGEOUSLY TAKING THE FIRST STEP
AND THEN THE NEXT STEP TOWARD ALL YOU DESIRE.

MEANT FOR MORE

My love for shoes began when I was only two years out of college and working at LaSalle Bank in Chicago.

Every day, I interacted with women who had gorgeous hair, gorgeous bags, gorgeous clothes, and gorgeous jewelry. And every day, I was transformed back into that seven-year-old, painfully shy and awkward little girl from Milwaukee, Wisconsin, who had a bowl cut and buck teeth.

To say I felt inept is an understatement. I struggled to find my niche in a world of confident, accomplished, beautiful women. I was insecure about my professional credentials and my personal style. To make matters worse, I was low on cash.

Will I ever belong here?

One evening after work, I stopped into a shoe store just down the street from my office. It wasn't fancy—just a sea of shoeboxes on folding tables with a display shoe carefully perched at the top of each pile. I would be lucky if I could pull out my size without disrupting the entire tower. Shoebox Jenga®.

I strolled between the tables, casually browsing, but didn't see anything of particular interest. I was there maybe fifteen minutes when I turned to leave—and suddenly, they appeared. A pair of shoes.

THE pair of shoes.

Cheaply made, patent-leather, black-and-white polka-dotted, slingback heels. If you looked close enough, you could see that some of the white paint had already flaked off the polka dots.

NEW STEP

I didn't care. They were $29. And they called my name.

I carefully slid the box marked 8.5 from the tower, removed the lid, and peeled back the tissue. I couldn't wait to slip them on. The heel was less than three inches tall, but it felt like a mile.

I set them on the floor, slipped my foot into them, and then bent over to figure out the slingback straps.

Is this where they're supposed to go?

I fumbled to get them on, but as soon as I stood up, something was different.

I was different.

I know that may sound trite. Or ridiculous. Or absolutely nuts. But it is true.

I stood taller. I felt more courageous. I took deeper breaths. I walked with more presence. This painfully shy, awkward wallflower suddenly commanded her space.

I had superpower. These high heels were to me what the web is to Spider-Man. The hammer is to Thor. The lasso of truth is to Wonder Woman.

In that moment, high heels became my secret weapon. I strutted to the checkout and took them home.

The next day, my heels quickly became the topic of conversation. I had found my niche and started building a collection of shoes that were affordable yet set me apart from the other women in the office.

I was, without a doubt, hooked on heels and the superwoman-like feeling I had every time I slipped them on.

My love for shoes and the fearlessness they gave me blossomed, and I continued to push the edge as to what I could (or should) wear to work while pursuing a corporate communications career. The more distinct the shoe, the greater my courage at work and in my personal life.

Brown patent-leather pumps with teardrop cutouts around the toes. *Sure!*

Lime-green suede mules with a peach bow on the front. *You betcha.*

White-and-yellow peep-toe block heels with a larger-than-life buckle that wrapped around the toe. *Absolutely.*

Black-as-night leather stilettos with dagger-like five-inch heels. *Hell, yes!*

With my high heels on, I continued to climb the corporate ladder and into the good life.

The Good Life

Fast-forward twelve years, and by all measures, I had made it! Life was good. I had a good career and income. Married a good man. Birthed two good kids. Lived in a good neighborhood in the good state of Colorado. Ate good food and drank good wine.

There was only one problem with my good life: I was slowly dying from it.

> *"When the personal soul life is burnt to ashes, a woman loses the vital treasure and begins to get dry boned as Death."*
>
> —Clarissa Pinkola Estés, *Women Who Run with the Wolves*

Every day was the same. I got up at the ass-crack of dawn and checked my phone to see what crisis had appeared overnight before I even crawled out of bed. I went downstairs to let out the dog and then back upstairs to the bathroom, resisting the magnet-like pull of my still-warm bed and sleeping husband. I begrudgingly turned on the shower, got myself ready, and then struggled to pick out an outfit. I woke up my sleepy kiddos to get them dressed. My three-year-old son woke up cheerfully and readily followed instructions. My eight-month-old daughter hated waking up and resisted me at every move. I ushered them downstairs and made breakfast, praying they wouldn't spill food on my clothes. I threw food into the cat and dog bowls and refilled their water bowl before I packed up the kids' things and then my things. I ran upstairs to wish Bill a good day and kissed him goodbye as he finished getting ready. Before walking out the door, I'd put on my high heels and muster up some superwoman power to get me through my day.

I struggled to fasten the kids in their car seats and set off for daycare. After walking the kids to their respective classrooms and giving them a kiss on the head, I headed to work.

I could do this routine in my sleep, yet it wasn't easy.

Some days, I took the long way or went through McDonald's for a Coke, just so I could have a minute or two to myself. Those days, one minute alone was more precious than a pair of Christian Louboutins.

Pulling up to the office building, I parked my car in the same spot and took a deep breath.

You can do this, Abby.

As I walked into the lobby and pressed the button for the elevator, I prayed no one would approach me. I was too tired to make small talk, but by the time I stepped out of the elevator, that fake happy smile was plastered on my face. I waved to colleagues as I made my way to my office, sat down at my desk, and plugged in my laptop.

Here we go again.

I looked at my schedule, which was packed with meetings.

Christ. I'm double-booked three times today.

I'd carefully craft excuses as to why I was not going to attend this meeting or jump on this call. I was already letting people down, and the day had just begun.

Fucking awesome.

I used to care about the bullshit. I'd even go so far as to say that I loved the bullshit. It made me feel important. I knew how to play the game, and I had made the varsity team. But suddenly, I was tired. I was over it. I was empty.

I went from one meeting to the next with to-dos piling up on the corner of my desk and in my notebook.

When the hell am I supposed to actually work?

After a day of pretending to feel important, I looked at my watch.

Fuck. It's 6 p.m.

I ran back to my office and grabbed my laptop, scrambled to the elevator, and frantically pushed the button a few times. I raced to my car and headed back to daycare, driving too fast in a desperate effort to make it before closing. I pushed open the doors and ran to my kids' rooms, apologizing: "I am so sorry. A meeting ran late."

Again.

I packed up their things, buttoned their coats, and struggled once again to get them in their car seats. The minute we walked into the house, I turned on the TV and plopped the kids in front of it. I let the dog out and raced upstairs to tear off my jewelry, kick off my heels, peel off my clothes, and throw on a T-shirt and a pair of printed pajama pants. Bill hated my pajama pants.

I raced back downstairs to figure out dinner, opening the refrigerator and then the freezer.

I really need to get to the store. Frozen fish sticks, boxed mashed potatoes, and peas it is, I guess.

While dinner was heating up, I checked my phone.

Shit. Forty new emails.

Hearing the garage door open, I breathed a sigh of relief.

Bill's home!

He calmly walked in the back door. The button-down shirt he ironed last night still looked pressed and was tucked into pants that hung perfectly over his polished shoes. He was tired too, but he greeted the kids with a big smile and gently kissed them.

"Daddy!" The kids adored him.

He strolled into the kitchen and gave me a hug.

"Nice pants," he teased. "How was your day?"

"Fine. How was your day?"

"Fine," he said as he walked upstairs to change in time to join us at the table as we sat down to eat.

After dinner, he cleaned up the kitchen while I bathed the kids and tucked them in. Once the kids were asleep, I went back downstairs and sat at the kitchen counter while Bill watched TV in the other room. I opened my computer and tried to keep from falling asleep; and when I could no longer see straight, I shut down my computer, walked into the other room, and kissed Bill good night.

I don't know how he stays up so late.

I walked upstairs, got ready for bed, and checked my alarm so that I could do this shit all over again the next day.

This was the good life.

Every day was a struggle.

And this was something not even the superpower of high heels could cure.

One minute, I was overwhelmed with guilt. *I have no right to feel this way. I am blessed with an amazing husband and two thriving, hilarious children. I have a good-paying job. I have a roof over my head. And I never go hungry.*

The next minute, I was consumed by anger. Pissed. I had worked my ass off to get where I was, and I felt like I was sold a bag of shit. *Is this all the Universe has to offer me?*

The next minute, I was overcome with sadness. *My children spend more time with their daycare providers than with me. And the time we do have together is spent rushing to a birthday party or sitting in the car dealership getting the oil changed or shopping for groceries. I never just sit and play with my kids. Bath time has become our quality time.*

The next minute, I was ashamed. *I half-ass everything. I half-ass being a professional. I half-ass being a mom. I half-ass being a wife. I half-ass being me. If I'm honest and do my math right, I quarter-ass everything.*

I was a pinball game of emotions. And I was tired.

Don't get me wrong. I absolutely loved parts of my life. There was just something missing. I needed something more . . . or something different. I didn't know what that looked like or what that was. I just knew I needed it. I desperately craved it.

MEANT FOR MORE

> *"In her unconscious, the desire for the red shoes, a wild joy, not only continues, it swells and floods, and eventually staggers to its feet and takes over, ferocious and famished."*
>
> —Clarissa Pinkola Estés, *Women Who Run with the Wolves*

This longing was constant. I couldn't turn it off. It was like a pilot light waiting to be ignited just below the center of my rib cage. At times, it burned orange and dim and gently simmered. Other times, it burned so blue and ferocious and hot that I swear it was going to burn a hole right through me.

I could numb this yearning during the mundane routine of the day. And by evening, I was so emotionally and physically drained that I had no energy to notice it. Literally, no gas to ignite the flame. But in the dead of night when all was still and I was somewhat rested, the fire reignited. It would start slowly, and although I was asleep, I could feel it grow until it burned so hot that it jolted me awake. I honestly don't remember how often this happened, but I do know it was often enough that I needed to do something about it.

How the hell am I going to keep living the good life AND satisfy this need for something more?

I strapped on a pair of high heels and set out to find the answer. This is the story of my journey—my epic quest for the Red Shoes.

I wrote this book for the woman who is dying of the good life. The woman who is tired of quarter-assing, has reached her tipping point, and is trying so hard not to stop in the middle of traffic, open her car door, step out, and yell at the top of her lungs: "FUCK THIS! I need something different."

I dedicate this book to you.

May you discover your courage and curiosity.

May you find your Red Shoes.

May you take the first step and the next step.

P.S. Throughout the book, I mention my quest for the Red Shoes. My definition of the Red Shoes varies quite greatly from Hans Christian Anderson, the Archer's and Dr. Clarissa Pinkola Estés— though I have quoted Dr. Estés earlier. I don't view the Red Shoes as an inner hunger that leads to obsessive, destructive behavior, but rather a desire that guides us to achieve our full potential. I liken the Red Shoes to Dorothy's Ruby Slippers: full of magic and power that lead us on a journey to discover who and where we are truly supposed to be.

THE "WRITE" STEP
YEAR 0 MONTH 0

"I'm starting a blog about high heels," I announced over dinner one Friday night.

No response.

My sweet, silent, round-faced, bright-blue-eyed daughter was tossing food from her high chair to my gentle, mild-mannered, food-obsessed adopted pup that resembled a border collie with the coat of a German shepherd, while my happy-go-lucky, joyful, blond-haired, blue-eyed son was singing a song he had just learned at daycare. Bill looked down at his plate with tired eyes and took another bite of whatever I had managed to whip up that evening.

Did they not hear me?

I had made the decision a few days prior in the hopes of quieting the storm inside. I liked to write, and I obviously had a thing for high heels. It was a brilliant solution, and I was ready to make it official.

"I'm starting a blog. And I'm naming it Mama's Shoes," I tried again.

My daughter clapped her hands because the dog was now begging for food. My son hummed the rest of the song, as he had clearly forgotten the words. Bill took a sip of water from his glass.

No response.

Have I suddenly become mute?

Finally, my mostly wonderful, sometimes-frustrating husband spoke. "When are you going to have time to write?" he asked before taking another bite. He didn't ask in a demeaning, snarky tone, but rather in a curious, matter-of-fact way.

I already had a full schedule with our daily grind. But in full disclosure, I was less worried about the time and more worried about the energy. And yet it didn't matter. I had made the decision.

There is no stopping this train. I have to do something, or I'll just fade away.

"I'll need one hour a week to write, and I'll do it after the kids go to bed. I'm dying to do something that makes me feel like *me* again."

"Okay," he said, smiling in my direction.

Bill worked in information security for a company he admired. He loved managing his teams, keeping up on the most recent threats, and learning the latest data-protection technologies. For the most part, he was content, but he always talked about owning investment properties that would generate enough income to replace his salary someday. I was envious that he had a long-term dream since the only dream I had was to stop the good life from slowing killing me.

Awesome. I'm starting a blog.

But there was one problem. I had no idea where to start.

Most Saturdays, I got up with the kids, fed them breakfast, and turned on a movie so the three of us could snuggle on the couch. Some days, we snuggled for the entire movie. Other days, we snuggled for two minutes before the family room cabinets and storage containers were completely emptied and it looked like Rainbow Brite had vomited on my white carpet.

Bill usually slept in. Part of me was pissed that he slept like a baby—which meant he rarely heard ours—so I was always the one getting up. Part of me was jealous that he could stay in bed so long. But most of me was grateful. This was the man who put up with my shit on a daily basis. He's the one who empowered me to live the good parts of the good life. And he's the one who built me a shoe closet in our first house.

Oh, how I really miss that shoe closet! I thought as I lay in bed, listening to the birds chirping just before the dawn broke.

THE "WRITE" STEP

I jumped out of bed as soon as I heard the footsteps in the hallway. It was my sleepy-eyed, wild-haired son. I hurried him downstairs, fed him breakfast, and turned on *Team Umizoomi*. Milly, Geo, and their robot, Bot, would keep him entertained for at least an hour.

I sat at the kitchen counter and looked at my laptop.

I have time to kill, right? Since only one child is awake, I only need to be in half-mommy mode. And Kid 1 is busy. Once Kid 2 gets up, I'll be in full-mommy mode. So . . . I'll just do one quick Google search.

I opened my laptop and Googled: "How to set up a blog."

So much for "after the kids go to bed," Abby. Nice.

There were thousands upon thousands of search results. I deliberately decided not to drown in a sea of information or overwhelm, so I just skimmed. Some of the information was helpful. A lot of it was junk. So I let my gut do the guiding.

Does this make sense? Does that sound like complete bullshit?

After a few articles and how-tos, it didn't seem that hard.

I can totally do this.

And I did. That afternoon.

While the kids took their afternoon naps, I snuck away to the basement bedroom and set up a free WordPress site, using a simple pre-built template. It wasn't fancy. But it was mine.

What image should I use? I paused, tapping my fingers on the laptop. And then it hit me. *Omg! That's perfect!*

A few months prior, I had stumbled upon an illustration of a flapper lady delicately holding a red shoe with a quaint black bow on the toe box.

I don't know how I found it. I probably Googled "high heel illustrations" or something similar.

This particular illustration resonated so deeply with me that I had to know more about it.

Turns out, the name of print was "Perfection." Vicky Scott, the incredibly talented UK illustrator who created this masterpiece, said it represented a woman's quest for the perfect shoe.

NEW STEP

Perhaps it spoke so loudly to me because it literally and figuratively represented my desire and my quest for the Red Shoes.

I emailed Vicky to ask if I could use the illustration as the profile picture for my blog. She loved the idea and granted me rights to use the image.

Just a few days after the initial inspiration, I officially launched Mama's Shoes.

I was venturing again into the wonderful world of shoes, and I came out of the gate with posts blazing. I was on fire, writing and posting a few times a week, smiling and laughing as I wrote about high heels. Frequency soon simmered to once a week, but I had thirty-six followers.

This is awesome!

I was having so much fun! And Mama's Shoes made me feel better.

I was no longer dying, but it didn't take me long to realize that not dying wasn't living.

Something was still wrong.

Vicky,

Your piece of work immediately spoke to me . . . and it still does! I absolutely LOVE it! Little did I know that those red shoes represented so much more than the perfect pair of heels. You are such a talented artist, and I am honored that you allowed me to use this masterpiece.

Ally Lou

PLODDING ON CRAIGSLIST
YEAR 0 MONTH 4

The desire was ablaze again.

I had kept it at bay with the excitement of Mama's Shoes, but the new blog smell was quickly wearing off.

I tried hard to ignore the thoughts. I scrubbed a little harder in the shower. I turned the music up a little louder in the car. I laughed a little longer with the kids. But nothing worked. The more I tried to extinguish it, the brighter it burned.

I had to admit it.

I am bored with corporate communications and sick of the corporate bullshit. There. I said it.

The career I had worked so hard to build for twelve years was now a big part of my problem.

And that, my friends, was a serious problem because I contributed 40 percent to our household income, investments, and plans for the future.

Get your shit together, Abby! You just need a hobby.

So while working full-time with two young kiddos and authoring a blog, I dove head first into helping founders of startups write and proof their business plans. Several of them had crossed my path by way of networking, and as I listened to them talk about their marketing and communication struggles, I just knew I could help them.

These founders wanted help. They needed my time. And I needed an escape.

NEW STEP

But there was one teeny, tiny glitch. I didn't know the first thing about writing a business plan.

So I opened my laptop, Googled "how to write a business plan," and got to work.

Sitting at the counter in our kitchen while Bill finished up the last of the dirty dishes, I was going on and on about how excited I was to be working with these startups: "This isn't going to take up that much time."

He looked up at me with his patient, but piercing, blue eyes and raised his eyebrows, not quite sure if he should believe me.

"I promise." I smiled, hoping he wasn't going to say it.

I fell in love with Bill because he was the first guy to tell me NO. The handful of gentlemen I had dated were kind, smart, funny, and motivated—except for one—but none of them told me NO. Bill was the first one to push me outside my comfort zone and call bullshit on my tough-girl persona. And when I tried to call all the shots, he told me NO.

Why isn't he telling me NO now?

"Can you take the kids to the trampoline park for three hours on Saturday?"

"Can I grab coffee with her on Sunday morning?"

"Can you pick up the kids on Tuesday because I have a dinner meeting?"

I asked these things of him without bringing home any additional income. This was volunteering (*errr . . . escaping*) at its best.

But it still wasn't enough to quench the desire inside, so I frequently browsed job openings for startups on Craigslist. I liked the startup energy—risking it all to follow a passion, a mission, a greater purpose.

I'm living vicariously through job postings on Craigslist. God, I'm pathetic, I thought and opened my work email so that I could trick myself into feeling important again.

It was a hot July evening. The kids had gone to bed, and I was downstairs in our finished basement. It was cooler down there. The sun hadn't set yet and the orange light was streaming in the windows when I stumbled across a posting for Natural Wellbeing Distribution and clicked on it.

PLODDING ON CRAIGSLIST

"A Vancouver, BC-based company that formulates and manufactures holistic supplements."

Cool.

"Operates two e-commerce stores."

Interesting.

"Looking for someone to help market and grow their flagship product—a hair supplement—both online and in retail."

Sounds like an interesting gig.

"Applicants need to draft a marketing plan."

Game on.

I had no experience marketing a consumer product, much less advertising and selling in an e-commerce environment or developing wholesale distribution channels. And I knew nothing about the health and beauty industry.

What the hell? I love a good challenge.

I replied that night, and the next morning, I had a response from Darcy Foster—the president. We set up time to chat, and after a brief phone conversation, I agreed to put together a plan for Hair Essentials.

After the kiddos went to bed that evening, I opened my laptop and Googled "how to market a consumer product."

Two days later, I sent Darcy a draft plan with suggestions on where to focus for the next ninety days and went to bed, feeling quite proud of myself.

"So when can you start?" he asked the next day.

Wait, what?

I wasn't serious. But he was.

Jokingly, I replied: "I would love to help, but you probably can't afford me."

Turns out, he could.

And suddenly, everything made sense.

Bill was now commuting ninety minutes each way to and from work, and while he liked his job, the good life was slowly killing him too.

NEW STEP

We were in the process of looking for a new house in a new neighborhood to reduce his commute, but we couldn't agree on a location. I was a stickler for good school districts. He was a stickler for being no more than thirty miles away from work. The only neighborhoods that fit the bill would flip our commutes so that I would be the one commuting three hours each day. Not an option.

If I take the job with Natural Wellbeing, I can work from home. No more corporate bullshit. The kids will still go to daycare full-time, but I can go to the grocery store at lunch. The dog will once again go on walks. And we can move.

But there was also a downside. Because the company was headquartered in Vancouver, I wouldn't officially be an employee. I would be a contractor. I'd have to establish a corporate entity, invoice Natural Wellbeing every month, and pay employer taxes. While I'd make the same, I'd bring home less. And I wouldn't have access to company-sponsored healthcare and retirement plans.

"This is an opportunity I can't pass up. I just *know* it," I told Bill late one night and waited for his response. I was on a work trip in Gettysburg and desperate to come home. I didn't want to do this anymore.

"But this is a big change," he replied. "Let's put together the budget impact and look at it."

With the numbers on paper, we agreed that this opportunity was worth the income hit and could be life-changing for us as individuals, as a couple, and as a family.

In August, I gave Corporate America the middle finger and became the Chief Marketing Officer for Natural Wellbeing Distribution. We also closed on a house in Superior, Colorado, that shortened Bill's commute from ninety minutes to nine minutes. And I dove head first into learning about e-commerce, online advertising, wholesale channels, and natural ingredients.

I was in heaven. I loved being more present for my family. And the desire inside had slowed to a manageable simmer.

PLODDING ON CRAIGSLIST

A few months later, I asked Darcy why he posted the job in Denver when the company was based in Vancouver.

"I don't know," he said, "It was just a gut feeling."

Well, here's to gut feelings.

I had found myself again, and I was learning about things I didn't even know existed: Google Analytics, Amazon Seller Central, influencer marketing, and online advertising.

With Darcy's support, I was winning and failing on a daily basis.

"I've come up with a new Facebook ad campaign," I started one morning on our daily video call.

"Perfect. Launch small and test it," he replied, taking a sip of coffee from his stainless steel travel mug.

"Do you want to see if first?" I wondered, not knowing the protocol.

"No, just do it," he said, checking his calendar to see if he was late for his next call.

"How'd the test go?" He leaned in closer to the camera two days later.

"It sucked," I admitted and slumped in my chair feeling defeated.

"Good," he said with a smile. "Now we know what doesn't work. Tweak the idea and re-launch." And we said goodbye for the day.

Such simple, brilliant concepts that did not exist in Corporate America, or at least the Corporate America I knew.

I was used to having to ask permission, justify every decision, beg for a budget, and explain away or hide failures. Perhaps the reason I hated my work in Corporate America was because it reminded me of that shy, awkward little girl from Milwaukee, Wisconsin.

NEW STEP

Darcy,

    You took a chance on me—someone you hardly knew who had very little relevant experience. This job afforded me the opportunity to live and breathe again. You encouraged me to get my hands dirty in e-commerce, social marketing, and online advertising. You empowered me to launch new products. You taught me the importance of testing, and how to fail gracefully. You showed me how to run a small business. You held me accountable like no boss before. And you laid the foundation for this incredible journey. Thank you!

A STRONG FOOTING
YEAR 0 MONTH 5 – YEAR 1 MONTH 9

I loved this new normal.

I slept until 6:45 a.m. and woke up the kiddos at 7 a.m. We ate without anxiety, and the typical screaming to get out the door had quieted to an occasional "Hurry up, guys!" The kids now saw Bill before they left for the day, and everyone was happier.

And the best part of the new routine was that after dropping off the kiddos, I came home and showered.

By myself.

In peace and quiet.

Showering in peace is worth the income hit! Every. Single. Penny, I thought as I enjoyed an extra few minutes under the hot water and then took my time getting dressed. I no longer stressed about what to wear. Some days were more casual than others, but whenever I had an important conversation or a big decision to make, I would always put on a pair of heels.

I loved walking downstairs to my first-floor office, opening up the French doors, sitting down behind my white desk and firing up my computer.

I thrived in this job.

I did things that were well within my wheelhouse, yet beyond my wildest imagination. I had never done this kind of work for a consumer product, but I did it all. Built new sales channels. Proposed product line extensions. Designed influencer partnerships and direct marketing campaigns. Monitored online advertising performance.

And I *finally* thrived in my most important job—mom.

"Guess what, Honey?" I asked my social, red-cheeked son when I picked him up from preschool.

"What, Mommy?" he replied with anticipation.

"I am going to the zoo with you tomorrow!" I was eager to see his expression.

"Do you get to ride the bus?" His eyes were wide with excitement.

"Yep!" I nodded and high-fived him.

"YAY!" he squealed and jumped into my arms for a hug.

Most evenings, I picked up the kids just before 5 p.m. and made an actual dinner. It was by no means gourmet, but it was planned. The kiddos played in the bath instead of being swooped out and dried off as soon as they were done. I loved watching the delight in my daughter's eyes as she poured water over her head. We were reading books before bed, and I loved listening to my son excitedly tell his version of the stories. I made it my mission to snuggle with each kiddo for ten minutes every night so we could talk about their day one-on-one. This was my favorite part of the day.

There is now more good than bad in this good life.

But things would soon change.

RUNNING TO THE NEXT
YEAR 1 MONTH 10

The weekend before Thanksgiving, we moved to Minnesota. It had been a short sixteen months since I accepted my position with Natural Wellbeing. Bill had been recruited to the Land of 10,000 Lakes, and since I could work for Darcy from anywhere, we packed up our things and headed north.

Of course, only the crazy or truly desperate buy or sell houses in Minnesota in the dead of winter, so we moved into a fully furnished corporate apartment and put most of our belongings into storage.

Cozied up in our two-bedroom place, I got back to work on Mama's Shoes.

Many nights, I laid in bed, browsing the latest shoes and searching for information while the kiddos slept and Bill watched *Top Chef* while ironing his shirts or folding the laundry.

In January, I posted an article about foot products that reduce pain and inflammation for women who wear high heels.

Are you kidding me? This is brilliant! I thought as I clicked "publish" on my blog post.

One was a spray that anesthetized the foot with Lidocaine. Another was a lotion that did the same thing.

Hang on . . . My hand clasped the mouse as it occurred to me.

Working for a company that formulates holistic supplements, I became acutely aware of the nasty ingredients in beauty products. And these foot products were no different.

NEW STEP

Really, Lidocaine? As in the drug-like numbing agent? Is it smart to numb a woman's feet, particularly when she's wearing high heels? Oh no! This is awful!

I reviewed the products in more detail and realized that there were less-than-ideal ingredients in most of them.

What are you going to do about it, Abby?

A new desire had been ignited. By the next afternoon, I'd made my decision.

I am going to formulate, manufacture, and sell a foot spray that alleviates foot pain and reduces inflammation for women who wear high heels—using only all-natural, organic ingredients.

Mic drop.

"Bill's going to love this one," I sarcastically whispered under my breath and rolled my eyes at myself.

I decided not to tell Bill and started prepping dinner.

"Hi, Honey. How was your day?" I asked when he walked in.

"Fine. How was your day?" He hugged me hello. Standing at the counter, watching him put down his things, I could see how much happier he was in this new job. Being second in command of Information Security at a Top 5 bank fit him well. So did the ten-minute commute. He had a little extra pep in his step, and it looked good on him.

"Good," I smiled.

Whew.

A few hours later, the kiddos had gone to bed, and Bill was sprawled out on the couch, reading the latest technology news on his iPad. He was wearing the blue pajamas he'd had since we started dating, and he looked the same, except his hair has changed from a brown to an Anderson Cooper-gray.

My incredibly handsome silver fox, I thought as I walked to the kitchen where my mind quickly jumped back to the foot spray. *If Darcy could launch a successful company focused on natural products, so can I.*

There was only one problem. I knew squat about formulating products.

RUNNING TO THE NEXT

So I opened my laptop and Googled "natural ingredients for alleviating pain and reducing inflammation."

This time, I was completely overwhelmed. My gut said I could NOT do this.

Perhaps this is a harebrained idea, even for me. I closed my computer, kissed my husband goodnight, and headed to bed feeling overwhelmed.

The next morning, I dropped the kiddos off at daycare and decided to take advantage of the corporate housing gym. It was a dated gym that had Dijon-mustard-colored walls and too much equipment.

No one's ever here. Why are there so many machines? I thought to myself as I squeezed by the stair-stepper and stepped onto the treadmill.

I am a walker. Literally.

My name is Abby Walker. And I hate running.

The only way I'll run is if I'm being chased by a bad guy!

I can't get the breathing down, I land heavy on my feet, and I can't control my arms.

But that morning, all of that changed.

The small TV was directly on the wall in front of me. It hung a little to the left but was too high for me to fix. It was muted and *The Today Show* was on. I put in my earbuds and turned on some tunes. This particular morning, I felt like EDM. (Mom: If you're reading, that's short for electronic dance music.)

As Afrojack and Steve Aoki's "No Beef" pounded in my ears, I started walking.

I increased the speed.

"I won't break down tonight . . ."

A little faster.

"I feel it for the first time."

Still faster.

"I found a new place here . . ."

My speed-walking turned into a light jog, and before I knew it, I was running. Like really running. And I didn't look like a baby bird trying to fly! I was coordinated and breathing with a consistent rhythm.

NEW STEP

Look at me! I am running!

And I ran for FIVE damn miles! It may not sound like a big deal, but this was huge!

This is a sign.

That morning on the treadmill, I knew anything was possible.

I am going to create this foot spray.

My gut said I couldn't do it. But maybe my gut was telling me I couldn't do it *alone*.

This dilemma kept me up (or woke me up) more nights than I care to remember. But my determination matched the intensity of the desire that burned inside.

I will find a way.

WALKING THE FLOOR
YEAR 2 MONTH 0

By March, Darcy and I had chatted via Google Hangout every weekday morning at the same time for more than a year and a half.

That's roughly four hundred video chats in a row.

I felt like I'd gotten to know him rather well.

His glasses were on. *Good, he's had his coffee.*

A slow blink. *I'll throw out another idea.*

Slight lean to the left. *His shoulder must be hurting again.*

He had become a tremendous teacher, mentor, and friend. When we finalized plans to meet at Expo West, a natural food and supplement tradeshow in Anaheim, California, I was so happy to finally see him in person!

He texted me so I knew what car he was driving, and as he pulled up to the passenger pickup area at the Santa Ana airport, I waved excitedly.

Chill out, Abby. You're acting like a giddy middle-schooler who's finally meeting her international pen pal.

Thing is, I was! I was meeting my international video pal.

His black mid-length, double-breasted trench coat was buttoned as he walked around the car to give me a hug. He was much thinner than I had imagined, but he wore perfectly tailored clothes and his blue eyes shone through his dark rimmed glasses.

"So good to meet you." His smile seemed even brighter in person as he held out his arms for a hug.

"So good to meet you." I smiled back, noting how strange it was to be in the same space with a person I'd only known via my computer.

NEW STEP

We were at the tradeshow for the next two days to determine whether we were going to exhibit at the venue the following year.

When we finished walking the show floor early on the final day, Darcy asked, "Want to grab an early dinner before heading back?"

"I'd love to, but I think I'm going to walk the floor again," I said with as much nonchalance as I could muster. You see, I was going to walk the floor again but with a different intention this time.

I am going to find a company to help bring my foot spray to life.

I didn't know the first thing about contract manufacturing, but before I left for California, I Googled "how to hire someone to make a product" and learned that contract manufacturers develop and manufacture a product under the brand of another company. My mission was to find a company that could formulate, manufacture, package, *and* label my foot spray. It was a pretty tall order, but I was determined.

"Okay, then. I'll see you tomorrow morning," he said as he offered another hug and then disappeared out of the convention center.

Alrighty, Abby! Let's do this!

Exhibitors were located in multiple buildings and covered a 350,000 square feet space, and the Health & Beauty section was located at the very far end. I really have no idea how to quantify the space, but it was big. Huge.

I'm sure I looked like a child who had just lost her parents at Disneyland as I turned in circles, taking in the energy and the noise. Delighted. Terrified. Ready to wet her pants.

To narrow my search, I had decided I would only stop at the booths that had sprays and liquids. I had no idea if this was the right approach, but it was my strategy. And I was sticking to it.

Sunscreens. *Keep walking.*

Lipsticks and glosses. *Not the one.*

Foundation and powders. *Nope.*

One booth stood out at the end of the last aisle. It wasn't the best-designed or well-lit booth, but it had sprays.

Spray moisturizers. Spray oils. Spray hydrates. This is the one!

I was terrified. Wishing I had worn high heels (or at least packed some in my bag), I channeled my inner superwoman and approached.

A fit, tall, and rather attractive gentleman walked toward me with his properly pressed light-blue button down.

Thank you, Universe. As if I am not intimidated enough!

I took a deep breath, looked up toward him, and then put it out there: "Hi. My name is Abby Walker, and I'm looking to create an all-natural, organic foot spray that alleviates pain and reduces inflammation."

In his thick French accent, he replied, "We'd love to help. Let me go get Dr. Paul."

Dr. Paul?

"Okay, great. Thank you," I stammered.

I soon found out that Dr. Paul is a former naturopathic physician from France who also dabbles in chiropractic treatment, clinical psychology, and pelotherapy.

I don't know what half of that means, but it sounds damn impressive.

A fiftyish-year-old man with salt-and-pepper hair, dark rimmed glasses, and a white medical jacket stepped out from behind the heavy, velvet green curtain that lined the back of the booth and shook my hand.

Dr. Paul.

[Insert French accent here] "Nice to meet you. What are you looking to do?"

Trying to sound intelligent, I explained my concept for the spray and how I needed help formulating, manufacturing, packaging, and labeling it.

He asked some really good questions, most of which I didn't know how to answer, and showed me a few of his spray products and bottle options.

Fifteen minutes later, we shook hands. "I'll be in touch soon," I promised.

If you are at all familiar with tradeshows, you know that fifteen minutes is a freaking lifetime. And I was truly impressed that he had spent that much time with me.

NEW STEP

This is my guy! I thought as I floated back to my hotel room, changed into my sea-foam-green pajama pants sprinkled with multi-colored hearts, and pulled out the notebook with emerald-green and gold foil stamping and a white day lily wrapped around the front and onto the back cover. I picked up the Holiday Inn pen on the nightstand and started writing.

And I didn't stop. In fact, I stayed up half the night brainstorming product names, doodling company logos, and writing advertising campaigns.

Abby, you're way too ahead of yourself. You haven't even told Bill yet.

I finally put the pen down around 2 a.m. and drifted off to sleep as I scripted the next big ask with my very patient husband.

TRIPPED UP

YEAR 2 MONTH 1

I could have flown myself home from California. That's how excited I was. Containing my excitement—or any emotion, for that matter—was something I'd never really mastered.

Heart, meet sleeve.

I burst into our corporate apartment like a fireball. "Bill! Bill! Bill!"

He was in bed, watching another episode of *House Hunters*. Ferrari, our light-gray, fully clawed, soft-as-silk cat, was asleep on my side of the bed. She always slept there because Bill had a nasty habit of unintentionally punting her across the room when he changed sleeping positions.

I sat on the edge of his side of the bed, rapid-firing details at my sleepy husband.

"So while I was there . . ."

"And Dr. Paul . . ."

"I think I want to name this spray . . ."

"Huh?" he said, his eyes widening a bit.

How is it possible that he didn't hear one word? Do I speak in a frequency that doesn't resonate in his eardrum? No one is that *good at tuning someone out.*

Maybe Bill has superpowers. Or just a lot of practice.

For the next two days, I drowned my husband in a sea of ideas and details. And as always, he patiently listened.

He is the tortoise to my hare. The ice to my fire. The logic to my emotion.

NEW STEP

One morning, as I poured the kiddos' cereal and juice, I pleaded, "This is something I *really* want to do."

"Do you even know how much it will cost?" he asked, as he finished packing up his lunch for the day.

"I don't have all the details yet," I admitted, as I looked up at him.

He put his hand over his face and slowly brushed his fingers across his forehead, down and around his cheek until the palm of his hand was over his mouth. At first, he didn't say a word. He didn't have to.

"Get the details, and then we'll talk," he sighed.

"Okay!" I tried to contain my excitement as I hugged him goodbye. "Have a great day!"

After the kiddos were in bed that night, I handed him my spreadsheet and the contract Dr. Paul had emailed me that afternoon.

"It's only $1,500," I said in a no-big-deal kind of way. We were under contract on a new house and were scheduled to do work on it after we closed, so even asking for $1 would have been a big deal.

His brow furrowed as he read the documents. "Okay, I'm on board as long as it's crystal clear that *you* own the formula once it's developed."

"Absolutely!" I agreed as I jumped up and down like a five-year-old who just got the go-ahead from their parents to ride the kiddy rollercoaster at the State Fair.

I don't know how I got to sleep that night, but the next day, a good dose of reality hit me as soon as I opened my computer and sent Dr. Paul the signed agreement.

I know nothing about product formulation or natural ingredients. Dr. Paul could send me fruit-flavored water disguised as an organic foot spray, and I wouldn't know the difference. Shit.

The sun streamed in and warmed my back as I sat at a high-top table in the community room of the apartment building. It was a bright room painted a soothing blue, and I was the only one who took advantage of the cheerful space during the day. I tried to work, but it was hard to ignore the impulse to reach out to Paulina Nelega, lead clinical herbalist at Natural Wellbeing.

A brilliant herbalist and natural health practitioner, she was a colleague-turned-friend, and I desperately needed her.

But what if she's pissed that I'm working on a side project? What if she says something at work? What if word gets to Darcy?

I gasped . . . *Darcy. Shit. I honestly feel like I'm cheating on him.*

And I didn't know if Paulina would feel the same way.

Paulina knew I authored a blog, and I often asked her opinion about products and picked her brain about ingredients, but this was different. This was *real.*

Despite my hesitation, I asked if I could hire her to review the formula and help me test the product.

"I'm so excited for you," she replied. "I'd love to help with the formula and review the samples."

Awesome!

Over the next few weeks, Paulina, Dr. Paul, and I formulated an organic foot spray that reduced inflammation and alleviated pain naturally. No artificial ingredients. No drug-like components. 100 percent pure.

And we nailed it!

This is an absolutely phenomenal product. Liquid gold!

But there was a problem. A big problem.

The foot spray fell apart when it was mass manufactured.

"Hi, Abby, the last samples we sent you were the same formula as the first one," Dr. Paul explained in an email. "There may be a difference because when we make very small batches, it is sometimes difficult to replicate the exact same effect; but as I said, it's the same formula."

Well, that's going to be a problem! I suddenly felt sick to my stomach and decided to call him.

"It's like baking," he said.

But I don't know the first thing about baking. Fuck.

"You can't just double or triple the recipe and get the same results."

Oh no. Now what?

NEW STEP

After a few more baking analogies, I hung up the phone and stared out the window at the spring plants that had just started peeking out of the ground.

I was stuck.

Stuck with this absolutely phenomenal product that I couldn't bring to market.

Stuck once again in the good life.

I shook my head and my eyes welled up with tears.

Darcy taught you better, Abby. You failed. So what? Try again.

Since I now owned the formula, I decided to get a second opinion.

After a quick search, and few phone calls, I found two other contract manufacturing firms that were willing to make samples of the foot spray.

I am not going to give up.

Paulina,

You kindly supported me through this foot spray venture, and while it ended up going nowhere, this series of events set me up for the next chapter in my journey. I admire you as a clinical herbalist and product formulator, and I am honored to call you a friend. Thank you so much for your support—then and now.

Abby Lou

CHANGE OF COURSE
YEAR 2 MONTH 2

One morning, I caught a glance of myself in the mirror hanging in the lobby of the apartment building as I walked to the community room to start the workday. I looked ragged and tired. The dark circles under my eyes were larger than normal.

Seriously, Abby, working full time, raising two young kiddos, and coordinating a move isn't enough to keep you busy? You're nuts! Almost certifiable.

I was physically tired, but I couldn't stop.

I hadn't asked Bill if I could spend more money on additional foot spray samples and wasn't ready to have that conversation yet. So I dove head first into market research.

I read everything I could about high heel pain, how high heels affect our posture and gait, why formulas fail . . . The list goes on and on.

You're exhausted, Abby. Take a break. Just one day off from this.

I had become manic. I was trapped in the quicksand of the good life again, trying to grab ahold of something. Anything. I tried this branch. It broke. I tried this root. It snapped. The blog, helping startups with marketing plans, and now developing a foot spray. I was sinking.

Desperate, my desire for the Red Shoes was once again raging.

Perhaps I was so fixated on this foot spray because I was looking for something to numb my pain. And the spray did exactly that.

Why are you looking for another escape? You have it REALLY good at Natural Wellbeing.

Yes, I did.

NEW STEP

But I don't want to work for someone else anymore. Not even Darcy.

I couldn't believe some of the stuff that raced through my mind these days.

I want to work for myself.

I had no idea where this was coming from.

The next morning, after dropping the kiddos off at daycare, I decided to walk a different way to the community room and found myself in the business center. It was a quiet, dark room with two round tables, each with four rounded-back leather chairs, and two desktop computers on a shelf desk hanging on the wall to the right.

Why am I here? Why am I not sitting at the high top tables in the sun?

I sat down at the shelf desk and signed into one of the desktop computers. Opening a new browser window, I Googled "high heel pain."

I'm certain I had searched those words before. Probably two million times. Yet I felt compelled to search them again.

11,500,000 results.

I started scrolling. Page 1. Page 2. Page 3.

Wait!

The words "Insolia® insoles" jumped off the screen and proverbially smacked me across the face.

I clicked the link, and it took me to a dated online forum. Half the ad images were broken and there was too much space between each post, so I had to scroll and scroll and scroll to follow the thread.

Two women were discussing their experience with Insolia® insoles, and it went something like this:

"Ladies, I just tried Insolia® insoles. LOVE them!"

"Me, too! They are amazing! They made some really uncomfortably high heels bearable for me."

"I am SOLD on these things. I've tried normal cushiony type inserts, and they really don't help the way these do."

"Totally agree . . . and they aren't that expensive. These insoles have changed the game."

Holy crap. What are these Insolia® insoles?

CHANGE OF COURSE

Back to Google.

"Weight-shifting insoles that redistribute the weight between the ball of your foot and your heel, so it feels more like you're walking in a flat and stops your feet from slipping forward."

I had a thousand questions.

Why have I never heard of these insoles?

Where can I buy them?

If they are as good as these women claim, do I really need my foot spray?

Shit. My foot spray.

My mind was racing and my desire was raging. Something inside me was lit up. I was terrified there may no longer be a need for my foot spray, and so excited by this newfound product that I could hardly contain myself.

I clicked on the "Contact Us" page and completed the form.

To whom it may concern:

My name is Abby Walker, and I am an avid high heel wearer and author of the blog, Mama's Shoes. I would love to learn more about your insoles. Please feel free to contact me at xxxxxx@gmail.com.

Kind regards,
Abby Walker
xxx-xxx-xxxx

Brian Hughes, Chairman & Director R&D at Insolia®, replied within minutes, and we scheduled a time to chat later that day.

I was so excited that I couldn't focus on Natural Wellbeing as I prepared for the phone call.

Am I really going to be talking to the chairman of the company?

I can't wait to learn more about this product!

Why am I so nervous?

The combination of anxiety and excitement rushed through me like I was a sixteen-year-old going on her first job interview.

I took a deep breath before dialing.

"Hi, Abby," he started.

"Hi, Brian. Thank you so much for speaking with me. I'm really excited about these insoles . . . and I haven't even tried them yet!" I laughed.

"That's great!" he laughed right along.

"I'd love to know more about them," I inquired.

"Let me start from the beginning," Brian began. His voice was soothing. His demeanor calm. Just listening to him eased my mind. My shoulders relaxed while he walked me through the history of the product. "In the late 1990s, New Hampshire podiatrist Dr. Howard Dananberg was challenged by one of his female clients to find a way to stop high heels from hurting. Though not a fan of high heels, he accepted."

Wow! This product has been around for a while!

"Dr. Dananberg was a pioneer in the in-shoe pressure mapping technology, and he discovered that most high heel pain was caused by pressure on the forefoot."

You don't have to tell me about forefoot pain. I know it all too well!

"He developed a prototype of an insole that ever-so-slightly rotates the heel bone up and back at the ankle to adjust the pitch and position of the foot in high heels so that the body pressure shifts off the forefoot to the heel," Brian continued.

Very cool!

"And because of my background in rocket science and engineering, a mutual friend introduced us, and I spent the next few weeks finessing Howard's design."

Wow! I've never talked to a rocket scientist before!

"When we launched the consumer version of our Insolia® insole, it became an instant hit." I could hear the excitement in his voice. "Women loved that it came in four different sizes so they didn't have to trim or modify it."

This is so interesting!

"At the time, they were sold in CVS and Walgreens. But after a few years, the buyers only wanted to carry one-size-fits-all insoles," he said with less enthusiasm. "We refused to compromise the science and dumb down the product to one-size-fits-all, so they stopped stocking the product."

That's really too bad, but good for you for not compromising!

"Since then, consumer sales have plummeted." His voice oozed disappointment. "Our focus now is designing and developing insoles that are manufactured into shoes."

Interesting.

"We still manufacture the consumer insole because it has performed well in the UK and parts of Asia, but US sales for the consumer product has quickly become our lowest priority." The disappointment seemed to have been replaced by resignation.

Oh no! Don't give up on this insole!

"Honestly," he continued, "we are considering exiting the direct-to-consumer market in the US. The only reason we maintain our online store is so our existing customers can purchase the product."

Please don't give up on it!

I could hear it in his voice that he was heartbroken. He had a product that could change the lives of so many women, yet no one knew about it.

He sighed heavily, "Getting this insole into the hands of US women is harder than building a rocket ship, Abby."

PLEASE! Don't give up!

Inside, I was begging him to not give up on the insoles as if he were suggesting giving up on me.

"Look," he admitted. "We're a bunch of MIT engineers and don't know how to market this product. If you have any ideas, I'm all ears."

Yes! Yes, I have ideas!

My mind raced. My heart beat faster. And the desire burned so hot that it could have set my shirt on fire.

"I don't think you should exit the market," I stated confidently. "In fact, I'd like to help you."

I had never tried the product. I knew nothing about the footwear industry, other than how to buy way too many pairs of shoes. But I had some very strong feelings about this insole.

NEW STEP

You're crazy, Abby!

"Really?" he asked with a bit of hope.

"Really," I said, holding the phone away from my mouth so I could gulp some oxygen and calm down my racing heart.

"Okay. I'll send you some samples, and we can talk again next week."

When I opened the package a few days later, I laughed at the perfect timing.

Bill had a conference in Las Vegas that weekend, and I was tagging along.

Vegas. The perfect place to test out a high heel insole. It doesn't matter if you're gambling, dancing, eating, or going to a show, heels in Vegas are killer.

I packed an incredibly uncomfortable pair of heels that always made me wince in pain after about two hours. I lovingly called them my Minnie Mouse shoes—platform red patent leather pumps with a round toe and a tan leather bow on the front.

As I write this, I have to laugh that I've never noticed the irony before. Of course, I would choose a pair of Red Shoes to test out these insoles.

After adhering the insoles, I slipped the shoes on.

I am going to give these puppies a run for their money. Because I never, ever take off my shoes. Ever.

I was the girl who wore white strappy stiletto heels at her wedding reception and who danced in those heels on the concrete floor for five hours, despite the excruciating pain. Two days later, I was in the doctor's office because I had bruised the tissue around my toes, which made it feel like my toes were disconnected from my feet.

I never took off my shoes.

Plus, I have to give these insoles a fair trial, right?

And boy, did I ever!

In the wee hours of the morning, we stumbled past the entry to the Michael Jackson ONE show on our way to the elevator at THE Hotel in Mandalay Bay, and I looked down at my Minnie Mouse heels in disbelief.

Why am I not in excruciating pain? I should be limping!

CHANGE OF COURSE

Normally by this time of the night (or morning), I would be in so much pain that I could literally feel the blood pumping through my toes. It was the kind of pain not even multiple margaritas could mask. I would curse every step and pray that a certain someone would offer me a piggyback ride. But Bill never offered. So I quickly learned that the trick was to keep moving. Never stop. Because if I stopped, I wouldn't start again.

So why am I stopping now?

"Ohhhh . . . that's a pretty glooooove," I said pressing my head against the glass of the Michael Jackson display case. "Do you think Michael Jackson wore thissssssss exact glove?"

Bill gently grabbed my hand and smiled at my slurs. "C'mon, Abby, let's keep moving."

We started toward the elevator, and I caught a glance of my red shoes in the door's reflection while we waited.

Why are my feet not on fire? Maybe those margaritas really did numb the pain? I bet they're gonna kill me tomorrow!

The next morning, I sat up, swung my legs over the edge of the bed, and braced myself for the high heel hangover—those incredibly painful first few steps.

Full body weight on both feet. *No pain.*

Step. *No pain.*

Another step. *Where is the pain?*

A full walk to the bathroom. *Could these insoles actually be magic?* I wondered to myself as I got myself ready for Day 2 in Vegas.

I had to be sure, so I put on the red heels and walked to breakfast and spent a good portion of the day walking around in the Red Shoes.

By the end of Day 2, I was dumbfounded and couldn't wait to talk to Brian the following week.

"They're magic, Brian! These things are incredible," I gushed. "I'd love to help you market these insoles. What do you think of me helping you in exchange for a cut of incremental sales?"

"Interesting," he replied. "Let me talk with the others, and I'll get back to you."

NEW STEP

Abby, when do you have time to market this product?

A few days later, he called me back. "Actually, Abby, we would prefer you become the exclusive distributor of these insoles in the US and Canada."

Wait, what?

"Yes!" The word flew out of my mouth, and my mind scrambled to process what had just happened. "Yes." I said again with more composure.

And with that, my education began. He was an open book. And I ferociously took notes.

"Last year, we made $40,000 on the product and barely broke even . . . The market is dominated by inferior products . . . Research indicates you cannot use the word comfort as comfortable shoes equals ugly shoes . . . Our studies show that these insoles will triple or quadruple the wear time . . ."

We talked for an hour, but I didn't hear a word he said. I was having a conversation with myself.

Me? An entrepreneur? Working for myself?

I knew zilch about licensing agreements. Next to nothing about managing inventory. And even less about financials.

Up until now, I was just a girl who loved high heels and was trying to manufacture a foot spray. Sure, I was planning to start a company some day, but . . .

I gulped for air.

Abby! This is it! A once-in-a-lifetime opportunity. Are you ready?

I wasn't the least bit ready, but I mustered up some courage and jumped in with both feet.

CHANGE OF COURSE

Brian,

   You shared every ounce of insight, every piece of research, every review, and every email address. You trusted me with your amazing product and handed me one hell of an opportunity. You are one of my biggest cheerleaders and one of my fiercest advocates. I cannot thank you enough for your generosity, your partnership, and your support.

Ary Lou

PAUSE TO REFLECT
YEAR 2 MONTH 2

I stood in the shower of our oversized corporate apartment bathroom the next morning. The kiddos were at daycare. Bill was at work. I turned the water temperature up to scalding—just the way I liked it. I honestly don't know how long I stood there, but I kept replaying how I ended up here.

I was never really much of a believer, even though my parents had always believed in God; and I was confirmed Methodist and married a Catholic.

As a kid, I was fascinated by The Big Bang theory and leaned heavily toward evolution. Of course, it went against what I heard at church, so I thought that made me a nonbeliever.

I did, however, believe that things happened for a reason—even the bad things. So on some level, I guess I've always believed in a greater force or a universal power.

As the water cascaded down my back, I started to connect the dots.

I fell in love with high heels.

I married a man who always supported my crazy whims.

I started a blog.

I volunteered with startups and learned to write business plans.

I was mysteriously and magically hired by Darcy and had a two-year crash course in product development, e-commerce, online marketing, and small business operations.

I wrote a blog post.

I had a wild-brained idea.

PAUSE TO REFLECT

I formulated a foot spray.

It fell apart.

I stumbled across a forum on which two ladies were chatting about an insole.

I reached out to the company.

The chairman replied.

And here we were.

I was being offered an opportunity to start a business that makes wearing high heels comfortable—that empowers women to channel their inner superpower.

Is there anything more perfect? And could my irrational amount of curiosity and slight bit of courage alone have led me here?

I leaned my head back under the water, allowing it to muffle all the other sounds, except the one in my head.

There is no way this happened by chance. I wouldn't have dreamed up this opportunity in a million years.

As I turned off the water, I also turned off all remaining doubt.

I couldn't help but believe that the Universe had been guiding me all along, and I was now being handed my very own Red Shoes.

Looking in the mirror, I noticed that the fatigue on my face had been replaced with the glow of possibility.

I knew my life was never going to be the same.

It's finally here, Abby. This is it. This is what you've been waiting for. Time to put on your highest heels and step into this amazing opportunity.

A GIANT LEAP
YEAR 2 MONTH 3

We were standing in the corporate apartment kitchen—a galley kitchen with a small closet at one end that housed the washer and the dryer.

The kiddos were tucked into bed for the night, and Bill was switching loads of laundry while I was gathering my courage. He pulled the wet clothes out of the washing machine and placed them in the dryer the way he'd done a million times before.

How did I get so lucky? A strikingly handsome husband that does laundry? I hit the jackpot!

I was leaning against the counter, my heart was pounding. I couldn't tell if it was from the excitement about this unbelievable opportunity or the anxiety of having to negotiate the details of the arrangement with Bill.

He knew I had spoken to Brian. He knew I had tested the insoles and loved them. He knew I offered to help Brian market the product, but I had not yet told him about the exclusive distributor opportunity. The one I had already said yes to.

I looked down at my hands, wishing I had drafted a speech and written the words on my palms for reference. And then I noticed my pajama pants—black knit pajama pants with orange and white stripes that had been washed so many times that the elastic waistband was stretched out, making the pant legs so long that now there were now holes at the bottom of each leg.

Why did I wear these? He hates these pajama pants the most!

It was too late. We were there. And we were having this conversation. Or at least I was going to try.

"So . . ." I started. "Yesterday, Brian offered me the opportunity to become the exclusive distributor of the insoles in the United States and Canada."

"Oh," he replied flatly.

I couldn't get a read.

Was that an "Oh?" as in "Cool. Tell me more"?

Or an "Oh," as in "I am exhausted and really can't process this right now."

Or an "Oh!" as in "Oh shit, Abby! Seriously? We're doing THIS again? We just closed on our new house and are in the middle of moving logistics hell, and you want to talk to me about a new whim of yours?"

He walked past me with a basket full of clean clothes, and I followed him and the fresh scent of laundry to the couch where he promptly turned on the TV and started folding laundry. I watched him carefully fold our daughter's size 2T shirts, and was overwhelmed with gratitude that he was such an incredible father and husband.

He doesn't want to have this conversation. Not tonight. Probably not ever.

I let it go.

But we both knew we'd be talking about it again soon enough.

I had already asked him for time.

I had already asked him for money.

And I had already asked him for his freedom, as we were solely depending on him for retirement and healthcare benefits.

All of these he gave up without question or hesitation.

I am just going to ask him for time and money—something we have successfully arranged before. This isn't any different, right?

But deep down, we both knew this was different. Very different.

At work, my husband is a masterful conversationalist, thoughtful negotiator, and compassionate people manager. In his quest to be a great leader, he has probably read *How to Win Friends and Influence People* more than a hundred times. Now that I think about it, I wonder if he was reading it to better manage his teams . . . or to cope with me.

. . .

I continued discussions with Brian over the next few weeks as if Bill had already said YES.

But he hadn't. Bill wasn't 100 percent sold on the idea. In fact, he wasn't even 1 percent sold. Because we still hadn't talked about it. We had just moved into our new home, and he was consumed with all things house and yard. And while we had not yet spoken of the opportunity, he knew I was consumed with all things insoles.

It was a lovely warm spring evening, and we were standing in the kitchen of our new house after the kiddos had gone to sleep. We loved everything about the kitchen, except the ridiculously small refrigerator.

Who would design a kitchen around this ugly-ass refrigerator?

I loved the black granite counters and fresh white cabinets. Bill loved the pantry layout and gas cooktop.

I took a deep breath, feeling grateful for this part of my good life, and quietly prayed he would be ok with the idea of me starting a company.

"So," I started. "I really want to talk to you about the insoles."

"Abby, I know you're excited about the insoles, and this is a tremendous opportunity to be the exclusive distributor, but I am nervous. *How* are you going to do this? How are *we* going to do this? Do you even know how to set up a company? Or how much money you need?"

"I haven't worked through all of the details yet, but I *know* this is an opportunity I can't pass up."

He didn't touch his face, which by this time of day showcased his rather attractive five o'clock shadow. He didn't roll his tired but beautiful blue eyes. He simply took a deep breath as if to say "here we go again."

"If it were just you and me, this would be a no-brainer," he confirmed. "But we really need to think things through so that we do what's best—for the kids and for us as a family."

He walked over and gently wrapped his arms over my shoulders and I wrapped mine around his waist. Sighing into my hair, he whispered, "I don't want to tell you NO, but you know I need some details. Put together a business plan, and then let's talk."

I squeezed him tighter and reached up to plant a grateful kiss on his cheek, fully aware that I was asking him to stretch beyond his comfort zone.

I went to bed that night, knowing this was all going to come together. I didn't know how, but I was going to make it work.

The next day, I dropped the kiddos off at school and daycare and rushed home to get some critical work items off my plate so I could get to the real work.

WHAT WAS MY BUSINESS MODEL?

I will purchase insoles from Insolia®. I will hire a warehouse to store and ship the insoles. And I will sell them to women who wear high heels.

This is probably THE most incomplete business plan ever, but I am too excited to worry about the details.

WHO WAS MY MARKET?

According to US Department of Labor statistics from a Women in the Labor Force paper, there are 72 million females in the workforce; 40.6 percent of which work in management, professional and related occupations (or 29 million women). And according to a 2003 "High Heels Survey" conducted by the American Podiatric Medical Association, 72 percent of women stated that they wore shoes with a 2-inch heel or higher (or 20 million of females in management or professional occupations). And of that 20 million, about 40 percent indicated that they wore high heels frequently. So

NEW STEP

I figured my target market was 8 million women—and that was on the conservative side.

Plus, as part of the exclusive distributor agreement, Brian was going to give me the email addresses of 18,000 women who had purchased or expressed interest in the insoles over the past ten years.

HOW WAS I GOING TO REACH THEM?

Email and online marketing.

HOW MUCH MONEY DID I NEED?

$7,500.

Honestly, I have no idea how much money I need. I know $7,500 is a big enough amount to purchase inventory, packaging, warehouse assistance, and a website. And a small enough amount to not trigger an automatic NO from Bill.

HOW SOON WOULD IT BE PAID BACK?

Based on my projections, three months.

I handed him the plan as soon as he walked in the door that night and wondered how long it would take to get his feedback.

The guy does not make decisions quickly.

Two weeks went by. Bill had not said NO, but NOT saying no was most definitely NOT a YES. He needed to say YES.

I tried so hard not to be that nagging child in the backseat screaming, *Are we there yet? Are we there yet?* But every night after the kids went to bed, I asked, "Have you made up your mind?"

And every night, the answer was the same: "Not yet."

WTF is taking so long?!

And then one night, he gave me the green light. Bill said YES.

Well, technically he said, "YES, *but . . .*"

"Abby, my biggest concern is time. When are you going to work on this? And can you guarantee that it won't negatively affect our family? Or your career?" His kind eyes were laser focused on me as we both leaned back on the black counters on opposite sides of the kitchen.

"I'll only work on it at night after the kids go to bed. I promise."

As soon as I said it, I realized Bill had heard that promise at least three times before: "I'll only write my blog posts . . . I'll only edit business plans . . . I'll only research ingredients . . . after the kids go to bed."

And I always failed on that promise. I shifted my weight uncomfortably and casually glanced out the window. I could no longer look him in the eye.

"I know you have great intentions, but I really need to know that you're going to keep your end of the deal. Why don't we draft an agreement between the two of us so that we are both on the same page?"

He is too good of a man to call me out. I shifted my weight again and stood up a bit taller.

"Okay, I can do that. I'll have one for you tomorrow," I agreed.

"Okay, now let's get some rest," he said, before kissing my forehead and heading upstairs.

The next morning, I went back to work and drafted a one-page contract, outlining and addressing all of his concerns.

After the kids had gone to bed that night, we walked in silence to the dining room table. I had placed the contract and a pen on the table after dinner was over, so we both knew why we were there.

He pulled one of the robin-egg-blue chairs out from the table, while I pulled out the bench and sat down directly across from him.

We didn't say a word or look at each other. He slid the paper toward him and started reading. Carefully. Slowly. This was a big moment. A HUGE moment.

I was giddy with excitement and nervous as hell.

Is this really happening?

NEW STEP

My palms started to sweat.
Will he really sign the agreement?
I started getting short of breath.
Will I be able to live up to all of the things I promised?
He glanced up, reached for the pen, and signed the contract.
OMG! OMG! OMG! He signed the contract. THIS IS HAPPENING!

PROMISES

We will evaluate after 90 days of operation and will decide whether or not to continue to pursue this online company.

Evaluation criteria to include, but is not limited to, the following statements:

- This new venture shall NOT interfere with or jeopardize Abby's day job.
- This new venture shall be fun and rewarding.
- This new venture shall break even within 90 days.
- This new venture shall NOT interfere with Abby's goal of losing weight and getting in shape (will work out).
- This new venture shall NOT interfere with family life.
- Abby cannot show signs of stress or frustration in front of kids.
- Computer will remain in basement while kids are awake.
- Family time may NOT be interrupted by business issues.
- This new venture shall NOT interfere with couple life.

He slid the signed piece of paper across the table so that I could sign it.

As I finished, I so badly wanted to scream, but I played it cool. We stood up from the table. He pushed in the chair, and I pushed in the bench.

Oh screw it!

I couldn't contain myself any longer. I jumped into his arms and hugged him tighter than I had ever hugged him before.

"Thank you so much," I whispered.

A GIANT LEAP

I was more nervous about signing this contract with Bill than I was signing the contract with Insolia®.

I cannot and I will not let him down.

LANDING ON A NAME
YEAR 2 MONTH 4

It took me a day to process what had just happened.

Bill had once again given me the freedom to pursue my Red Shoes.

God, he's a good man, I thought as I opened my laptop.

I was nervous as hell, but I was ready to go.

But there was one problem. Bill asked that I open a credit card under the business, so that I could track the $7,500 of "approved" business expenses separate from our household expenses.

Staring at the first page of the online credit card application, I shook my head.

Shit. A business name. I don't have a name!

I didn't know the first thing about naming a business. So I opened another tab and Googled "how to name a business."

Most of it sounded like complete bullshit: "It should be one word." "It should have the letter 'x' in the name." "It should be five to ten letters long and have at least one hard consonant."

What a load of poop!

For the next few days, I struggled with what to name the company. I took the dog on longer-than-usual walks, hoping to get some inspiration. I turned up the radio and danced a little crazier, hoping that a few great ideas would jostle to the top of my mind. I quickly cooled the water in the shower, hoping to shock a company name into existence.

Nada.

LANDING ON A NAME

I wanted to give this company a personality, and I thought the best way to do so was to give it a *real* name—one that captures the essence of the women I wanted to serve.

Determined to find a name, I headed downstairs to the dungeon of an office because per our agreement, that was where all work related to this business was to occur.

Bill and I shared an office in the finished basement. To the right of the basement stairs, there was a hallway that led to the utility room and one large long room that we used as a media and toy room. To the left of the stairs, there was a sitting area and a bedroom.

It wasn't a nice bedroom, as it just had a little vent window up toward the ceiling that let in one stream of light that blinded me every time I walked in the room.

Damn, that's bright!

The walls were a grocery bag tan color, and the carpet was a deep forest green. It was a plush, thick carpet with randomly placed speckles throughout the design.

Which speckles are supposed to be there and which speckles are crumbs? I often wondered.

The office had a good-sized closet with white bifold panel doors that were too wide for the closet opening, so when you closed the doors, they didn't shut all the way. It was like a big W shooting out from the wall.

Bill's ginormous executive oak desk was pushed up against the wall to the left. It was designed to be a corner desk, but there was no room for two desks if we made it a corner desk. So we lined up all three pieces against the wall. It literally was all desk from one side of the room to the other.

He had installed a ceiling fan for circulation, but in doing so, we lost the large overhead light in the already-dark room. There were lights on the fan, but they were little. No matter how many watts we stuck up there, it was still barely light enough to read.

Thank goodness for these lamps, I thought as I turned all five of them on. Yes, it took five lamps to light the room!

NEW STEP

Floor lamp. Desk lamp. Lamp with little shades. Lamp with huge shades. Lamp without shades.

I tried my best to feng shui the space. I had been feng shui-ing (*is that even a word?*) our houses ever since I read *Move Your Stuff, Change Your Life* about ten years prior.

I don't know if I do any of it the right way, but I try!

I sat down at my oversized white desk and started brainstorming the characteristics of my ideal customer, hoping that a name would emerge.

> She stands tall and shines bright.
> She graciously accepts a compliment with a simple thank you.
> She has an opinion—and rarely wavers from it.
> She is striking in the way she carries herself.
> She refuses to be ignored or left behind.
> She is an active participant in everything she does.
> She is a free spirit but a rule-follower when necessary.
> She is just the right mix of courage, sass and determination.
> She keeps good company.
> She loves to laugh.

I leaned back in my chair, satisfied with the list, but disappointed that a name had not yet magically appeared.

At dinner that night, I thought it would be fun to get Bill's perspective. "What name comes to mind when you hear these characteristics?"

I read them to him slowly.

"Easy. You're describing Vivi." With a proud-Daddy smile stretching across his face, he glanced in her direction.

Holy shit. He's right.

I had just described our three-year-old daughter, Vivian Louise.

Why didn't I think of this? It's so glaringly obvious.

As soon as dinner was over, I sprinted downstairs to the basement, and started searching domain names.

vivianlouise.com. *Not available.*

vivilouise.com. *A pinup model and makeup artist.*

vivianlou.com. *BINGO. I had my company name.*

Vivian Lou. *It's perfect. I love it!*

I immediately registered the domain name (using another credit card I kept to track any personal expenses for Natural Wellbeing) and applied for a Vivian Lou credit card.

Bubbling with excitement, I barely felt my feet touch the ground as I made my way upstairs.

It will be here in a few days, and then I can get this party started.

When it arrived in the mail, I ran downstairs to the basement to open it.

I am more excited about opening up this envelope than I was about opening up college acceptance letters!

I couldn't get the envelope open fast enough and threw the torn paper like it was confetti.

My very first business credit card!

I held it up to get a really good look at it, and then I saw it and nearly lost my breath.

The card's expiration date was Vivian Louise's birthday.

This is a sign.

I sat down in my desk chair, closed my eyes, and gratefully whispered to the Universe, "Thank you!"

ONE FOOT IN FRONT OF THE OTHER
YEAR 2 MONTHS 4–6

The changes were subtle at first, but I started to un-numb. I breathed a little better. I smiled a little bigger. I laughed a little louder.

And soon, I was in full execution mode. Morning mom. Daytime career woman. Evening mom. Nighttime entrepreneur.

I'd created a ritual of dropping the kiddos off in the morning and swinging by Caribou Coffee for a medium Northern Lite Vanilla Latte, even though I was never much of a coffee drinker. I liked the smell, but I didn't like the taste much until our realtor introduced me to the Northern Lite Vanilla Latte a few months prior. We were on one of our marathon house-hunting missions, and it sent jolts of energy through my veins.

A little extra boost of superwoman.

I was hooked. I didn't know what was in it—nor did I care.

That's ironic coming from the girl who was upset about a little Lidocaine in her foot spray, I thought to myself as I reached through my car window for the delicious drink.

I loved that *finally*—at the age of thirty-six—I had joined the big girl's club of coffee-addicted professionals.

Steaming coffee in hand, I walked into the house and straight downstairs and prepped for my day.

At 10 a.m., as I did every morning, I hopped on my Google Hangout call with Darcy.

"What are you working on today?" Darcy asked curiously as he adjusted his glasses.

"I'm going to track down all of our hard costs for Hair Essentials and develop wholesale pricing so we can start reaching out to salons and spas."

"Great plan," he smiled.

Whew. He approved.

It felt good. While I loved this freedom, I wasn't used to it and found myself seeking guidance and approval. Just like I had done in Corporate America. Just like I had done as a kid.

"Alright, I think I have everything I need to get started. See you tomorrow!"

"Great! Til tomorrow!"

I closed my chat window and worked until 4:45 p.m. and then signed off to go pick up the kids and enjoy my afternoon and evening Mom Routine. Dinner. Baths. Books. Bedtime.

After the kiddos went to bed, I hunkered down and devoured as much information as I could. By 9:30 p.m., I could hardly keep my eyes open, so I kissed Bill goodnight and went to bed.

I slept like a baby until 2 a.m., the time when the burning desire in my chest woke me up every night.

No sense in trying to sleep. There is a lot to do.

I tiptoed downstairs, fired up the computer, and got back to work on Vivian Lou.

I had very limited knowledge. And that's being generous. I honestly had no idea what I was doing. Not a freaking clue.

So you bet your sweet ass I Googled . . . everything.

E-commerce platforms
Legal entities
Trademarks
Licensing contracts
Minimum quantities
Purchase orders
Insurance
Branding

NEW STEP

Packaging
Kitting
Fulfillment
UPC codes
Pricing
Credit card processing
Website development
Email platforms
Banks

In June, I selected an e-commerce platform.

The extent of my HMTL knowledge was limited. I knew how to bold words and hyperlink text, so I found a plug-and-play platform that processed credit cards on my behalf. I didn't want to build something from scratch, and Shopify seemed like a good option.

In June, I also pored over agreements and contracts.

Okay, I'll be honest. My dad pored over the legal documents. These agreements could have requested that I relinquish all parental rights for my firstborn child, and I would have signed them.

In July, I created a legal entity.

Since I already had a relationship with a tax accountant, I relied heavily on her suggestion.

In July, I also set up a bank account.

I didn't want any hassle or extra fees, so I Googled best banks for small businesses. Luckily, one of the options had a location in Minnesota!

Boom!

That month, I also toured warehouses and fulfillment centers.

If it's up to me to put the insoles in a box, pull orders, and ship inventory from my basement or garage, this business is doomed!

The only way this would work was if I had a partner to box up my product, house my inventory, and fulfill orders. By the grace of Google, I found a fulfillment center forty minutes away from my house that would take on a small startup AND was a Shopify expert.

Done.

In August, I agonized over logos.

To some, logos mean very little. To me, the logo was a big deal. Maybe because it made this company real? Maybe because it was my daughter's name? So I called on Jeff Forrest—a designer who was a referral from a referral who had helped me with several projects at Natural Wellbeing. He was so excited and drafted several logo concepts, free of charge!

"Edie, which one of these two do you like better?" I asked my mother-in-law, who was in town with Papa for two weeks in August to see the kiddos.

I am sure this is how she envisioned her vacation—helping her daughter-in-law pick out logos!

"Ummm . . . I like this one!" she said.

She probably just selected this one to get me out of her hair. But that's totally fine! We're going with it!

In August, I designed my own packaging.

I have to get this done cheap.

I called a handful of packaging designers who blew my budget right out of the water. So I went with an online firm that sent me the die-lines of the box (Mom, if you're reading this, die-lines are the shape and dimensions of the package), and I designed it myself. You gotta do what you gotta do! I had the boxes shipped to my warehouse so they could assemble the final product.

And then I partnered with organizations dedicated to helping disadvantaged women.

I wanted to donate a portion of every sale to organizations that helped women revitalize their confidence and reclaim their independence, so I decided to partner with Dress for Success–Twin Cities (MN) and Women's Bean Project (CO).

I just love these charities!

I also placed my first purchase order.

NEW STEP

I had no idea how to place a purchase order. So I copied a template, modified my information, and sent it to Insolia®. I placed an order for 2,400 insoles.

And then I struggled with pricing.

I spent a good chunk of time researching pricing. Should it end in a .95 or a .99? Should I offer a single pair or a multi-pair? Insolia® was selling three pairs for $24.99, and there was no way I could maintain that price and be profitable.

"I think you'll want to continue to offer bundles," Michael Backler, President of Insolia®, offered during a Google Hangout.

"And I think you'll probably want to keep the price as close to the existing price, so as to not alienate our existing customers," Brian added.

Something about offering multiple pairs at a low price felt wrong. I didn't want to compete with the drug-store brand of insoles, but who was I to question anything? I took the lead from Insolia®.

In September, I customized my e-commerce store.

Because my budget didn't allow me to hire a designer, and I knew basic HTML, I wasn't afraid to modify my site. I browsed sites that I liked, found their source code, copied it into my template, and modified it with my content.

This isn't pretty, but it gets the job done.

That month, I also took my own product pictures.

This isn't amazing, but it gets the job done.

And wrote my own copy.

This isn't perfect, but it gets the job done.

And trademarked my name.

This was more expensive than I had budgeted, but it was something that Bill insisted I do.

It was a lot of work, but it wasn't impossible or overly complicated. I did most of it in the wee hours of the morning and during a few stolen hours when Bill took the kiddos to the park.

It was exhausting, but oh so exhilarating!

This is all for ME!

ONE FOOT IN FRONT OF THE OTHER

Physically exhausted, but still wide-awake at 4:30 a.m. every morning, I popped a few Anxiety and Stress Essentials supplements and headed back to bed.

By the time I pulled up the covers, my pulse had slowed and the burning in my belly had cooled.

Damn, these Natural Wellbeing products are G.O..O…D….!

I finally slept.

By the end of September, I was ready to launch.

Here goes nothing!

Mom, Lizzy, Amanda, and Rachel,

You listened, reviewed, read, edited, and provided your opinion when I bent your ear on all things Vivian Lou. You could have told me to shut up; you could have changed the subject; you could have rolled your eyes, but you listened patiently. I love you!

avry lou

Jeff,

You didn't owe me anything, but you gave me my brand. It's such a seemingly "simple" logo, but that logo represents far more than a company or even my daughter's name. It was my opportunity to do something bigger, step outside of my comfort zone, and take a chance on an unbelievable opportunity. Thank you for designing the perfect logo and for making me laugh. To unicorns!

avry lou

JUMPING IN

YEAR 2 MONTH 7

It was 5 a.m. on a Friday in October.

Despite a healthy dose of Anxiety and Stress Essentials, I couldn't sleep.

I quietly crept downstairs and grabbed Duke, our ten-week-old kitten that my now kindergarten-aged son, William, had found lost on the side of the road, from the laundry room. In the last month, Duke had become my constant companion and confidant. Liberty, my loving pup, followed us to the dungeon office.

I need all of the support I can get!

Still in my pajama pants—the light pink ones with flamingos in the shape of a heart—I fired up my laptop and removed the password from the site.

VivianLou.com was now visible to the world.

It's LIVE! OMG! It's LIVE!

There was no launch party. There was no popping of champagne. It was just me, a dog, and a kitten. I leaned down and high-fived (or high-pawed) Liberty. I did a little chair dance, and they wagged their tails to celebrate with me.

And then I sent off the following email.

From: Abby Walker
To: Abby Walker
Date: October 3 at 5:56:28 AM CDT
Subject: I'm jumping in . . . with my high heels on!

JUMPING IN

Hello family, friends & colleagues!

As most of you know, I have a very healthy obsession with stilettos, pumps, and all things high heels.

And that is why I am so excited to launch my own company selling products designed to increase a woman's confidence when it comes to wearing heels.

Yes. You read that correctly!

I am opening an online store dedicated to helping women look + feel better in high heels.

It's a bootstrapped startup so I am launching with one product—Insolia® Insoles for High Heels—a high heel insole that redistributes body weight between the ball and heel of the foot resulting in better balance, straighter posture + less pain. I plan to quickly expand the store to include organic foot care products (starting with an organic foot spray to alleviate pain + reduce inflammation for when high heel pain sets in), and non-toxic shoe care products, among others.

The company will donate a portion of every sale to organizations that help disadvantaged women regain + sustain confidence in their personal and professional lives. The organizations I've selected are Women's Bean Project in Denver and Dress for Success in the Twin Cities.

I am so excited (+ nervous + scared + happy + relieved + hopeful + on and on)!

So without further ado, I introduce Vivian Lou. www.vivianlou.com

Thank you so much for the support, encouragement and kind words I've already received from so many of you!

Here's to jumping in with my heels on!

Love!

Abby

p.s. If you are interested in trying the insoles, I've set up an introductory Friends + Family coupon! Use code **JUMPINGIN for 25% off.**

NEW STEP

Later that afternoon, I received an email from Brian.

From: Brian Hughes
To: Abby Walker
Date: Fri, Oct 3 at 2:59 PM
Subject: Fwd: Order confirmation for order #1012

Abby:

I am in Europe with my mother who is about to have a cataract operation, and I was planning on showing her your draft site and surprise, it's LIVE! I've placed an order to see how the process went—so far so smooth.

Good luck on the launch. If there is anything I can do to help please let me know.

All the best,
Brian

Oops! In all of my excitement, I forgot to include Brian and Michael from Insolia®!

Despite that massive oversight, it was a great day!

I checked my store ten times that day to see how many sales I made and before I headed up for the night, I ran down to the basement to check it just one more time.

"Bill!" I yelled as I ran up the stairs. "I made fourteen sales and $378 today!"

"Amazing! Congratulations, Honey," he quickly replied and returned to watching *Hell's Kitchen* reruns on Hulu while drawing out how he was going to install CAT-5 ethernet in every room of the new house.

I was so incredibly proud and excited as I floated upstairs to get ready for bed. As I finished brushing my teeth, I looked at myself in the mirror and caught a glimpse of the pure joy that was radiating from within.

I just made $378 in sales on my first day. This is going to be awesome!

I crawled into bed and fell asleep, dreaming of what was possible.

MISSING THE MARK
YEAR 2 MONTHS 7–9

I woke up the next morning and many mornings after with one question on my mind: *So where does one start finding new customers when they've just launched an e-commerce company?*

I responded to Help A Reporter Out inquiries. *Got a few small media mentions.*

I tried my hand at Google AdWords. *Epic failure.*

I tested a few Facebook Ads. *No response.*

Well, thank goodness for email marketing and Brian's contact list.

With Brian's help, I planned to email the list of 18,000 women who had previously expressed interest in the product or purchased the insoles from Insolia® in the past. But there was one problem: these women purchased three pairs for $24.99 from Insolia®, and I was now selling two pairs for $19.95.

I was nervous. Really nervous.

Getting the women to purchase from Vivian Lou is more important than making money right now, I told myself when I saw Brian's email.

"How do you want to do this, Abby?"

His question was simple, and I suddenly had a simple answer.

"I'll offer a 40% discount when they buy from me and will honor that discount for the next six months. How does that sound?" I replied back, not knowing if it was a good approach or not.

"Okay," he responded nonchalantly.

NEW STEP

"I'm thinking we should send the emails out in waves to test the message and timing of the email," I suggested in my next reply.

"Good idea," he agreed.

The first email went out to 1,000 women on October 19. And it worked!

I made $311 in sales.

The second email went out to the next 1,000 women on October 21. And it worked!

I made $457 in sales.

OMG! I am in business!

By mid-December, we had exhausted the list of 18,000 women. In three months, 541 women had subscribed to my email list, and I had made 539 sales, totaling $13,500 in revenue. I had covered my start-up costs.

I wasn't making much profit (or any profit, to be quite frank), but it was okay.

It's just a hobby.

And I didn't sign my name at the bottom of the emails because I was too scared to associate with the company, but it was okay.

It's just a hobby.

And I didn't dare update my Facebook or LinkedIn profiles, as future employers might question my loyalty to corporate communications if they saw that I was the President and CEO of a startup on the side. It was okay.

It's just a hobby.

"It's just a hobby" became the mantra and eventually a convenient excuse.

I didn't put myself out there. I didn't pitch my product. Heck, I didn't even ask for the sale.

I set up daily and weekly Google Alerts for a variety of high heel and insole-related terms and often looked to those for email content inspiration. And I started sending an email to my 541 subscribers every Sunday. While it contradicted what I'd learned from Google, Sundays were my best-performing email days with higher open rates and more sales. So I stuck with it!

MISSING THE MARK

Every week, I wrote about something related to high heels—how to prevent blisters, stretches to keep feet in good shape, and tips on how to prevent pain—because I still struggled with making "the ask."

I always added a "p.s." at the bottom of the email that went something like "p.s. If you want to prevent swollen, tired, aching feet due to high heels, be sure to add Vivian Lou Insolia® weight-shifting insoles to your shoes."

Every Sunday morning was the same. I got up early, slipped downstairs into the dungeon of an office, and logged into MailChimp to put the final touches on an email I'd already read 1,000 times.

All was quiet, and I was nervous. My palms started to sweat, my stomach began to churn, and I could feel (almost hear) the pounding of my heart.

Why am I so damn nervous?

I took a deep breath, moved the cursor over the 'Send' button, closed my eyes, and clicked.

I quickly opened my eyes to confirm I had clicked the right button, high-fived the MailChimp monkey hand, and exhaled.

In December, my mom replied back with: "Loved your email today. So funny and so you!"

She was always one of the first to open and read my Sunday morning emails, I thought before reading the next line.

"But you didn't ask me to make a purchase. Abby, when are you going to start asking people to buy your insoles?"

I gulped as I sat there without an answer. *Good point.*

For some reason, I had a huge resistance to making "the ask," which is just a slight problem when you run a company that sells goods.

Seriously, Abby. Why can't you sell?

I closed my computer that night and decided that I was going to figure out where the resistance was coming from, and then I was going to kick its butt with one of my favorite high heels.

SHUFFLING ALONG
YEAR 2 MONTHS 10–11

"Why don't you find a co-working space?" Darcy suggested during one of our morning video chats. "It will be good for you to be in a different environment and meet new people."

This wasn't the first time he'd suggested this. He knew something was off. I was distracted. I wasn't as enthusiastic as I had been in months past. I was slower than usual in replying to his emails. And I was no longer suggesting new ideas. I was simply going through the motions.

I don't want to do this anymore. I want Vivian Lou to take off.

"Yeah, that sounds like a good idea," I said, smiling back at him. We finished our morning chat, and then I went to work finding a good space.

I found a great one just across the street from Vivian's daycare. It was the kind of space with a variety of configurations—booths, cubicles, small tables, and chairs by the fireplace. I paid a monthly membership fee so I could use the conference rooms, small phone booth-like rooms for private calls, and the color printers.

This is actually perfect! And the attached café's vanilla lattes aren't half bad either. They aren't Northern Lite Vanilla Lattes, but they will do.

The Natural Wellbeing Hair Essentials wholesale channel was growing quickly. I spent quite a bit of time interfacing with our new retail partners, and continued to call on large spas and salons to see if they were interested in carrying the product.

But I was scared.

SHUFFLING ALONG

I picked up the phone and dialed the next prospect. *Please don't answer!* I pleaded as the phone rang and my throat tightened. I hated talking on the phone, much less asking for the sale while talking on the phone.

This whole not wanting to "make the ask" issue is now haunting me at work too? Great.

Not being able to sell Hair Essentials was not okay. It had become a central part of my role. And *this* was not a hobby—this was my job, my livelihood, my part of the contract with Bill.

Spa Shiki in Lake of the Ozarks, Missouri, was next on my list. I picked up the phone and called Spa Director, Ann Brown.

My palms started to sweat as soon as she answered the phone, but my anxiety subsided quickly as we chatted. This conversation was different.

She was kind, interested, curious about the product . . . and she placed an order!

I didn't even have to ask!

There was something about Ann. She and I had this uncanny connection—kindred spirits of sorts. Over the next few months, we talked about business—how to better market Hair Essentials and possible product line extensions. We talked about family—our husbands, our children, and recent vacations. But there was something we didn't talk about: Vivian Lou.

Since December, sales had consistently slowed. January sales totaled $2,050. February totaled $1,300. And March totaled $900.

I was worried. My credit card debt was rapidly accumulating, and I wasn't selling enough to cover my expenses.

What the hell am I doing wrong?

So I Googled "how to build an online business."

Based on the results of my search, I started following people like Steve Chou, Ezra Firestone, Amy Porterfield, Nathalie Lussier, and Marie Forleo. Steve and Ezra had successfully launched physical product e-commerce companies and were now teaching others how to do the same. Amy was an online marketing expert. Nathalie was known for helping entrepreneurs grow their email lists. And Marie Forleo was an inspirational powerhouse.

NEW STEP

A few weeks into my online education, I wanted to enroll in Marie's B-School—an eight-week online program for people looking to create a life and business they loved. But it was a lot of money.

"Bill," I asked one night, unsure if I should sign up for the course. "Are you okay if I put an additional $1,999 on my credit card to take this online course?"

He hesitantly agreed, and I enrolled that night.

The next day, I grabbed a piping-hot vanilla latte from the cafe and sat in one of the booths by the front windows. I plugged in my headphones, opened up my binder, and started the modules.

Truthfully, I devoured the content, religiously watching all of the videos, and completing all of the assignments. (Thank goodness for those colored printers at the co-working space!)

There was a lot to learn in B-School, but it was Marie's philosophy behind marketing and selling that completely flipped the script for me.

"If you have a product or service you believe in—one that truly helps others—it's your responsibility to do everything you can to market and sell in the most effective way possible. Because if you don't, you're stealing from those who need you most," she claimed.

My responsibility? Market and sell in most effective way? Otherwise, I'm stealing?

Ouch. That statement hit me. Hard. And it was just the kind of wake up call I needed.

Abby, it's time. This is on YOU. Step up. Stop hiding. Start marketing.

It began to occur to me that while Vivian Lou was a crash course in all things business, it was also a crash course in all things ME.

Why do I have such resistance to making "the ask"?

Why am I sabotaging this amazing opportunity?

Why do I feel completely and utterly unworthy of this business and of being successful?

Why am I so afraid of money?

What the hell is wrong with me?

SHUFFLING ALONG

These realizations surfaced unexpectedly and quickly as I watched others in the B-School community thrive in their businesses, and I was overwhelmed with panic.

In all my previous jobs, I could hide from doing the things that made me uncomfortable. I could reprioritize work to do the fun and easy things. But now, with my dream on the line, I had to figure my shit out.

I am not going to throw in the towel. I am not going to steal from those who needed this product most. And I am sure as hell not going to leave my family in debt.

I needed to do something, but I didn't know what.

And not even Google could help me this time. *Seriously, what would I search? "What's my problem?"*

As I leaned forward on the desk and rested my forehead in my hands, I felt compelled to call Ann.

I reserved one of the private rooms at the co-working office. It was a small, closet-like room. I slid open the frosted glass door, stepped inside, and slid the door closed behind me. The walls were painted a rich sky blue color and an off-white shelf desk hung on the wall to the left. I sat down on the black mesh desk chair, took a deep breath, and dialed Ann.

"Hi, Ann? It's Abby. Do you have a few minutes?" I asked, noticing that my voice was a bit shaky.

"Of course, Abby. What's up?" I relaxed at the kindness of her voice and then quickly diverted from my intention for a few minutes. I asked her about the spa, and how Hair Essentials was selling, before I began my confession.

"Ann, I want to tell you about something I'm doing in my free time—a business I started on the side . . ." I began.

"Okay great," she encouraged.

I spent the next few minutes verbally vomiting over the phone. About the insoles. About Vivian Lou. About my lack of sales. About my self-limiting beliefs.

"Hey, Abby . . ." she stopped me.

"Yes?" I was glad she interrupted my insanity.

NEW STEP

"I'm starting my own company, too." I could hear her smile on the other side of the phone.

"What?!" I exclaimed and sat up in my chair.

"I've just launched Saltibility—a Himalayan salt company—and I know exactly what you're going through."

I breathed a sigh of relief so heartfelt and so powerful that I'm surprised it didn't blow down the frosted glass door.

She continued, "I'm going to give you the names of two people. Meet with them. They may do you some good."

Yes! I'll do anything. I'll meet with anyone. I need to get out of my own way!

She gave me the names of a life coach who specialized in nutrition and an Emotional Freedom Techniques (EFT) practitioner.

I scheduled a video chat meeting with the nutritionist life coach a few days later and didn't feel much of a connection.

Plus, I eat fine (minus my extreme addiction to all things chocolate!).

Sitting forward determinedly in my chair, I moved on to EFT.

Emotional Freedom Techniques? What the hell is that?

I Googled "EFT":

"Removes internal resistance that limits success so you can gain emotional freedom to pursue being, doing, and having what you want."

Yes, please!

I leaned forward in my desk chair and kept reading:

"Negative self-limiting beliefs are usually formed in early childhood when we interpret events. These interpretations become beliefs and reside in our subconscious as blocked energy."

This is a bit of a stretch, but I'll go with it.

I settled back into my chair.

"Like acupuncture and acupressure, tapping along the body's meridians can chip away at [these blocks] to clear emotional discomfort, stuck negative emotion, and dysfunctional patterns of self-judgment."

Sounds interesting.

SHUFFLING ALONG

"By following specific verbal scripts while tapping, we reframe our interpretation of past events, allowing us to change how we feel and behave, and what we believe."

Okay, now this is little woo-woo even for me.

I slumped into my chair, wondering if this was a good idea.

What the hell do I have to lose? I asked myself as I closed my computer, packed up, and headed across the street to pick up my little Vivi. By the time I started the car, I knew the answer.

Nothing. I have nothing to lose by reaching out to this guy.

> Ann,
>
> We've never met in person and haven't spoken in years, but I've closely followed your success with Saltibility and am so incredibly happy for you. While the time you spent in my life was just a few months, the impact you made will last a lifetime. You took an interest in Hair Essentials when I needed sales, you took an interest in Vivian Lou when I needed an ear, and more importantly, you took an interest in me at a time when I desperately needed help. You knew I was struggling far more than I admitted, and I would have never tried EFT without your suggestion. Your encouragement and recommendation forever changed my course. I consider you a guardian angel, and have no doubt that we were meant to cross paths. I hope to meet you in person one day so that I can give you a hug, look you in the eye, and thank you for changing my life.
>
> *Avery Lou*

CATCHING MYSELF FROM FALLING
YEAR 3 MONTH 0

The next morning, I dropped the kiddos off like usual and headed to the co-working space. I tried to work. I tried to watch the B-School modules. But I couldn't concentrate. I was fixated on figuring out myself.

By mid-afternoon, I headed home. I had to get to the bottom of my issues, and I desperately wondered if EFT could help.

I pulled out one of the robin-egg-blue chairs from the dining room table, opened up my laptop, and started typing. And typing. And typing.

Whoa, Abby. I can't believe you poured all of that into an intro email. It's quite insightful, but you sound a bit desperate.

I sat back in my chair, wondering if this was all necessary.

Ummm . . . yes, I am desperate.

Send.

From: Abby Walker
To: Greg Oldenburg
Sent: Thursday, March 12 at 2:50 PM
Subject: Referred by Ann Brown

Hi Greg!

I received your name from Ann Brown—a customer + colleague who has quickly become a friend! She and I spoke today about our new ventures, and I asked her who she would recommend as a life coach. She mentioned that instead of a traditional life coach to consider meeting with you!

CATCHING MYSELF FROM FALLING

To be quite honest, I am struggling with a host of self-limiting beliefs.

I am the oldest of four girls and come from a relatively privileged background. My parents put me through college and subsidized my graduate school. I am 37 years old and have started my own company (www.vivianlou.com). I also work full time remotely as the Chief Marketing Officer of Natural Wellbeing Distribution (www.naturalwellbeing.com). I am in a sometimes challenging, but overall wonderful + supportive marriage. I have two wonderful kiddos. So on the surface, everything LOOKS great. And IS great—except for me. Ha ha!

FOR YEARS (since I can remember), I've struggled with something inside of me that says I don't deserve success, I am not smart enough. People can see through me and think I am a fraud. I don't deserve to have money (or fight for a promotion or pay raise).

It is SUFFOCATING, and it's more apparent now that I am starting my own business.

I have good ideas and valid opinions, but I am afraid to voice them. I know I am smart enough to run/grow my business, but I do not and cannot picture myself being successful or hiring people to work for me. It's almost as if I am paralyzed to grow and be successful.

I don't know if it's my perspective on myself or my perspective on money.

All I know is that I want help! Ha ha!

Do you serve "remote" clients? I am located in Minneapolis. If not, can you recommend someone who is local?

I look forward to hearing from you.

Thanks!
Abby

I didn't hear from Greg that night.
I wonder if he's busy.
I didn't hear from Greg the next day.

NEW STEP

Shit. Did I share too much and scare him off?

I finally heard from him the next day.

Whew!

Turned out he doesn't check his email frequently, and he preferred to communicate via text.

No worries! I can text.

We set up time to chat the following week, and I was really nervous.

Are you sure you want to do this? I asked myself repeatedly.

But the "you have nothing to lose" argument always won out.

I didn't know if I was nervous because I was about to share my fears and issues with someone I'd never met, or uncomfortable with the idea of "tapping" in order to unblock energy, or perhaps deep down I knew that something significant was about to happen.

But at the end of the day, it didn't matter. I was desperate and determined.

> Greg,
>
> When I look back at this email, I laugh a little. I dumped quite a bit on you in this first introduction. Thank you for not running for the hills. Thank you for replying back. And thank you for embarking on one hell of a journey with me.
>
> Avy Lou

TAPPING INTO SOMETHING
YEAR 3 MONTH 0

"So . . . tomorrow I have my first session with this new business coach," I announced to Bill just before heading up to bed.

I referred to Greg as my business coach because I honestly had no idea how Bill would react if I told him I was going to call up some random guy, tap on parts of my head and chest, and repeat phrases he said to me in an effort to clear stuck energy.

He would probably freak out. He already thinks I'm nuts for wearing natural deodorant.

"Good," he replied nonchalantly. "I hope it goes well."

He didn't ask any further questions. I didn't offer any further details.

The session was scheduled for 2 p.m., and I was so nervous that I left the co-working space after hanging up with Darcy.

When I got home, I Googled "EFT tapping sequence" and again watched YouTube videos of people tapping.

Holy shit, this is weird.

At 1:50 p.m., I walked upstairs.

Where should I make the call?

I decided to make the phone call in our master bathroom with the door locked.

God forbid Bill comes home and sees me doing this.

I sat down on the cold tile floor and leaned up against the off-white vanity cabinet doors. After I positioned myself in the slight stream of

NEW STEP

sun that shone in from the window, I leaned my head back and looked at the ceiling.

What am I doing?

I checked my phone. 1:55 p.m.

I closed my eyes and took a few deep breaths, reminding myself of what I was doing and why.

I'm doing this for my own good. I need help. I know this because I wouldn't have sent that email otherwise.

1:59 p.m.

I couldn't wait any longer. I dialed his number.

My palms started to sweat, but I didn't plead for him not to answer.

RING . . .

Please pick up.

RING . . .

Please pick up.

"Hi, Abby," he started. "It's so nice to meet you via the phone."

Whew!

His voice was gentle, nonjudgmental, and kind.

"So nice to meet you, too," I said, feeling some excitement.

After a lengthy talk about my past, my present, and my desired future, we started the session.

"Remind me again where I'm supposed to tap?" I asked.

"On the top of your head, start of your eyebrow, side of the eye, under the eye, under the nose, your chin, your collarbone, and under your arm. Take your time, Abby. Let me know if you need me to pause."

I'm so glad he's on the phone so he doesn't have to see me struggle to get these moves down.

"Repeat after me," he coaxed and then proceeded to guide me through one of the oddest experiences I've had. After our one-hour call ended, I felt relieved. Thankfully, EFT wasn't as weird as I thought it was going to be, and I was feeling a subtle shift in my body.

We set up a time to speak the following week, and it soon became a standing meeting.

TAPPING INTO SOMETHING

"What's been going on this week? How are you feeling?" Greg would start each session.

I'd answer honestly. "I'm frustrated about this. I'm mad at myself for this. I am feeling a lot of resistance to this."

Some sessions were more intense than others, but I always felt liberated and a bit lighter after our calls.

Maybe this IS working.

About a month into my sessions with Greg, I realized my issues ran far deeper than I thought.

I had handcuffed myself with a whole host of limiting beliefs, and I had to work hard to clear these blocks if I wanted to get Vivian Lou off the ground.

I was soon meeting with Greg twice a week to battle the internal demons that said: *I am not worthy.*

It wasn't easy, but I could feel subtle changes, and that compelled me to stay the course.

I'm going to keep this up until I can sell these insoles without any resistance!

WALKING AWAY

YEAR 3 MONTH 1

B-O-R-I-N-G! I thought as I reluctantly opened yet another spreadsheet.

The priority at Natural Wellbeing had shifted from building a wholesale channel to growing sales through Amazon.

At the time, we had more than 250 products in our portfolio, and I was drowning in spreadsheets. I was now responsible for ensuring our listings contained accurate keywords and product details.

I hate spreadsheets.

So not only was I distracted, I was now disinterested. Really disinterested.

And Darcy knew it.

"What do you want to work on, Abby?" Darcy asked in late April when I expressed my disinterest in Amazon spreadsheets.

"I don't know," I replied, uncertain of how to answer since what I really wanted to say was, "Vivian Lou."

"Think about it, and let me know," he said. "We'll make it work, even if that means cutting back your hours or looking at a new arrangement."

Why is he so nice? I would have fired me months ago!

One night after the kiddos went to bed, Bill and I sat on our large white faux leather couch in our family room, facing the TV, though it wasn't on. Only the kitchen light over the sink was on, so it was dim enough for him to not see the tears that started rolling down my cheek.

"I hate this. I'm no longer happy at Natural Wellbeing, and I feel like I'm cheating on Darcy again. I so desperately want Vivian Lou to work out."

"I know, Honey," he said and put his arm around my shoulders.

"What do I do?" I said as I turned to cry on his shoulder. The quiet tears soon turned into a full-blown sob.

After a few minutes, he said, "Why don't you quit?"

I stopped sobbing and looked up. "What?"

"Why don't you quit Natural Wellbeing and look for a corporate communications job that you can do with your eyes closed? That way, you can work on Vivian Lou and not have to stress about spreadsheets or sales."

"Are you being serious?" My eyes were wet and wide with surprise.

"Would I say it if I weren't?"

Nope. Bill never says anything he doesn't mean.

I went to bed, relieved and a little sad.

The next morning, I opened up my Google chat, took a deep breath, and said it: "So Darcy . . ." Tears welled up in my eyes. "I'm giving my notice."

The tears now streamed down my cheek as I told him how unhappy I was working on Amazon spreadsheets, how excited I was about launching Vivian Lou, and how desperate I was to make it work. I told him I planned to take a few weeks off and then look for another job that I could do in my sleep.

"I'm so sorry, Darcy," I said unable to look him in the eye.

"Don't be sorry, Abby," he consoled. "This is really exciting! I wish you the best of everything."

"Thank you, Darcy," I started. "You have been one of the best mentors I've ever had."

When my last day arrived, we agreed to stay in touch, and I ended the video chat feeling sad . . . and so much more.

NEW STEP

Holy shit! I just quit the best job I've ever had . . . and one that allowed me to work from home! What the hell am I doing? Now I have to make Vivian Lou work.

I took a deep breath and walked out of the basement office with a bit of sadness, and a hell of a lot of determination.

PEP IN MY STEP
YEAR 3 MONTH 2

After dropping the kiddos off at daycare and camp, I returned home, Northern Lite Vanilla Latte in hand, threw open the French doors to the three-season room, and took a deep breath.

Why does cedar smell so good?

Spring was now in full swing, and I was in love with the room just off the kitchen and family room. It was a cedar wood room with a vaulted ceiling. The walls were lined with six-foot windows and a sliding glass door to the patio. It overlooked our extremely overgrown garden, and the sounds of the birds and scratches of the squirrels soothed my soul.

We hadn't yet purchased furniture for the room, so I set up a folding table, a folding chair, and an extension cord and called it my new office.

This is the perfect spot for me.

I opened my laptop and checked Indeed.com and LinkedIn for any new corporate communications listings that met my requirements: paid well and easy as hell.

Nope. Nothing. Nada.

Then I got to work on Vivian Lou.

Sales were still slow. April sales totaled $1,500, and I was on track to make $1,200 in May.

These insoles are amazing. It's me who is not. It is my responsibility to get them in front of the women who need them, and I'm just not making it happen. Why isn't this EFT stuff working faster?!

NEW STEP

I spent most of the month updating things that I thought were important.

I changed the words and images on the website.

I redesigned the packaging. And by redesign, I mean changed some words and added a sketch of a high heel (yes, I even sketched it!). It was still an inexpensive brown cardboard box.

And I wrote emails. Lots of emails.

These tactics were working, but not well enough.

While I believed in the insoles, I started to question my ability as an entrepreneur. I'd stare at other entrepreneur's websites. *They are so successful.* I'd watch other CEO's YouTube videos. *They have it all together.* I'd drool over other brand's social media accounts. *They're so good!*

After hours of comparing myself and Vivian Lou to other entrepreneurs and brands, I'd slump backward in my chair, pull my legs to my chest, and bury my face in my knees. I was too dignified to lay in the fetal position under my desk so I sat in the fetal position on my chair.

I SUCK!

Deep down, I knew I should spend more time doing than comparing. Why was I comparing myself to entrepreneurs who had been in the game for six years when I'd only been in six months? Why was I watching YouTube videos if it was never a channel I planned to use? And why was I not using the other brands' social media accounts as inspiration instead of performance benchmarks? I could have used this time to create, test, and try something new, but instead, I ended up in the fetal position . . . over and over again.

I worked with Greg on some of this. I worked with myself on some of this. And I worked with Rachel Platten on some of this.

"Here's Rachel Platten's chart-topping 'Fight Song,'" Ryan Seacrest announced over SiriusXM radio.

Yes!

I leaned over to crank up the radio as I turned down my street.

PEP IN MY STEP

"Like a small boat
On the ocean
Sending big waves
Into motion..."

I sang at a moderate volume.

"This is my fight song
Take back my life song
Prove I'm alright song
My power's turned on..."

My volume increased.

"But there's a fire burning in my bones
Still believe
Yeah, I still believe..."

Goosebumps shot up my arms and I now shouted at the top of my lungs.

"Starting right now I'll be strong
I'll play my fight song
And I don't really care if nobody else believes
'Cause I've still got a lot of fight left in me."

I pulled into the garage with a renewed determination, walked straight upstairs to put on a pair of high heels, and then headed back to the three-season room to get to work.

Vivian Lou will be successful. I will be successful.

A GUIDING LIGHT

YEAR 3 MONTH 3

I sat at the folding table in the three-season room, enjoying my Vanilla Northern Lite Latte, and decided to log into Facebook before checking LinkedIn or Indeed.com.

There was a notification from a Tena Pettis, who posted a message in the Minnesota B-Schoolers Facebook group. It wasn't an active Facebook group, so I was surprised by the notification and curious as to what this Tena lady had to say.

"I have an event I am hosting with my coach and mentor this Friday. I would love for you ladies to join us! I believe we have five more spots + it is free! Ursula helped me more than double my sales in less than six months. She has a unique approach to sales and one I believe all of us online biz owners need to grasp on to. You can register here."

Double your sales? I'm in.

Free? Hell yeah!

Only five more spots? Shoot! I hope I'm not too late.

I registered immediately and secured a seat.

The morning of the event, I woke up in a panic.

I asked Bill to take the kiddos to daycare and camp so I could get ready and not have to fuss with the morning schedule. He agreed. Those days, Bill and I didn't talk much about Vivian Lou. He knew I was trying my best, but wasn't selling enough to cover expenses, and I was always defensive whenever he inquired about progress. In the name of marital harmony, it was best we not go there.

A GUIDING LIGHT

So what does one wear to a free seminar for entrepreneurs? As the CEO, do I wear a suit? Are jeans too casual? UGH!

I wore brown slacks, a purple shirt, and a jean jacket, completing the outfit with my favorite pair of brown patent-leather heels before heading out.

I hope this Ursula lady is the Superwoman Sales Expert Tena claims she is!

I was relatively new to Minnesota and relatively new to entrepreneurship. Plus, I had worked from home for the past three years, so I was relatively new to (or getting reacquainted with) in-person adult social interaction. I was nervous as I pulled into the hotel parking lot.

I took a deep breath and walked into the Radisson Hotel. I followed signs to a conference room just to the right of the lobby, which I found packed with ladies greeting each other with hugs, laughing, and reminiscing about previous events.

Deep breath, Abby. You got this.

I found an open spot three chairs in from the left of the second to last row.

Perfect!

The event started and Tena introduced Ursula Mentjes as a sales expert and certified sales coach who helps her clients double and triple their sales.

She stood about six feet tall and wore a navy blue dress with nude colored heels. *Love that she's wearing heels!* Her long, perfectly curled blonde hair fell over her shoulders as she shared that she was a farm girl from Minnesota, but lived in California. I smiled, thinking that she exuded both states in perfect harmony. She spoke for the next two hours, sharing her Seven Secrets to Selling.

I was mesmerized and could not write fast enough.

"Set your intention to find the fastest and easiest way to your quantum sales goal. Expect to see business growth, and start calling. I promise you, you don't know enough to mess it up. If you set the intention, it will happen."

She was generous with the information she shared.

NEW STEP

"Your prospects, clients, and customers aren't going to call you back. You need to call them again and again. 81 percent of sales close after the fifth call, and only 10 percent of sales people make the fifth call. If fear weren't an issue, how many times would you call?"

She was gentle but firm in the advice she had for business owners.

"Don't be afraid; be of service. Don't be scared; be helpful."

Her approach to selling was so damn effortless.

This lady knows her stuff.

While most of the tips were for businesses calling on prospects, it was easy for me to translate this tough love to online sales. Selling finally made sense to me.

She finished the session by inviting us to Sales Camp—a two-day sales intensive event—in late June. I so badly wanted to sign up on the spot, but $999 was a lot of money. A lot. I had just spent $1,999 on B-School, and I had not yet recovered that investment.

I lingered in the room, torn about to what to do, and made small talk with a few fellow attendees who sat by me. And then she approached.

"Hi. I'm Ursula. Thank you so much for coming today." She held out her hand.

"Hi. I'm Abby Walker. I sell insoles for high heels," I blurted.

"Interesting. Tell me more." Her smile was warm, and her attention was solely focused on me while I briefly told her about the company and the product.

"Cool. How much do you sell them for?" she asked.

"Two pairs for $19.95."

She looked me directly in the eyes and, in the nicest voice, said, "You're underpriced."

What did she just say?

I raised my eyebrows, thinking I had misunderstood her. "What?"

"You should be charging $24 per pair." She said it as if she had extensively researched the insoles and knew this with absolute certainty.

Is she being serious?

I giggled nervously and mumbled, "I can't charge that."

"Why not?" Her smile widened.

"Because Insolia® used to sell three pairs for $24, and it is a stretch for me to sell two pairs at $19.95."

"Who are your competitors?" she coaxed.

"Dr. Scholls®, but not really. This is a far superior product." I stood up a little straighter at the thought that my product was so bad-ass.

"Okay. So why are you priced like Dr. Scholls® then?" She raised one of her eyebrows in a very kind challenge.

Hot damn.

"I don't know," I shrugged.

"If $24 makes you nervous, sell one pair for $19.95. See what happens." She took a step back, as if her work was done.

"Okay, I will," I smiled.

Wait. Did I just agree to double my price?

"When do I make the change?" I asked.

"Tomorrow." She smiled gently and walked on to the next lingering attendee.

Holy shit. Why am I totally at ease with this complete stranger—who doesn't know me nor has ever tried the product—telling me to raise the price?

I didn't have an answer.

I spent the weekend replaying the conversation in my head. *Did that really happen?*

Bill was totally on board. He loved the idea.

So on Monday, I called my warehouse and told them to reassemble my packaging. I was now selling one pair for $19.95. They needed to take out one pair of insoles from each box and use a black marker to cross out the words '2 pairs' on the front of the packaging.

There's no going back now, I thought as I hung up the phone.

They needed a few days to schedule the job and complete the work.

On Friday, I updated my website.

And on Sunday, I sent the following email to my 1,071 subscribers.

NEW STEP

From: Abby Walker (Vivian Lou)
To: Abby Walker
Date: Sunday, Jun 7 at 4:59 AM
Subject: Price increase + a personalized discount code.

Loyal Vivian Lou customer:

I am writing today to let you know that after very thoughtful consideration, I am raising the price of Vivian Lou Insolia® insoles.

The price increase is due to continued investment in research on how best to prevent and reduce high heel pain, as well as the development of new products.

Vivian Lou Insolia® insoles will now retail for $19.95 per pair.

As a loyal customer and subscriber, **you will be able to purchase Insolia® insoles at the current price (2 pairs for $19.95) through September.**

Your unique discount code is: ABC123DEF456

Use this code to buy one, get one free at www.vivianlou.com until September 30.

Vivian Lou Insolia® is the best investment you can make when it comes to preventing high heel pain.

Here's why.

Vivian Lou Insolia® is the ONLY high heel insole scientifically proven to PREVENT high heel pain. It is designed to:

Adjust the pitch + position of feet in high heels.

Shift weight off the ball of the foot.

Stop feet from slipping forward.

Improve ankle stability.

Straighten posture.

It permanently adheres to the inside of your shoe, and unlike foam insoles (that sell for up to $24.95/pair) or gel insoles (that sell for up to $29.95/pair), Insolia® insoles:

A GUIDING LIGHT

Don't need to be replaced every 6 months.

Don't harbor odor or bacteria.

Don't go under the front of your foot.

Don't absorb and disperse the stepping motion energy, which ironically, causes foot and back pain.

And are impossible to see in open-back and open-toe heels.

With Vivian Lou Insolia® insoles, you can wear the high heels you love—without the hurt.

I sincerely thank you for your loyalty, and I am honored to have you as a customer and supporter.

Thank you,
Abby

OMG! I just doubled my price AND flawlessly pitched my product.
It didn't feel slimy. It didn't feel sleazy. It felt right.
I only received two emails from disgruntled customers.
Two out of 1,071 isn't bad!
The next day, I signed up for Ursula's Sales Camp.

HIKING THROUGH CAMP
YEAR 3 MONTH 3

"Good morning, Sales Campers," Ursula said, standing tall at the front of the room, wearing another navy-blue dress and another pair of nude high-heel sandals.

She must wear this blue color for a reason. I wonder what it represents?

I had decided on a white linen knee-length skirt with blue embroidery, paired with a white T-shirt, a jean jacket, and a pair of gray high heel mary janes. I made a conscious decision that morning to avoid calling too much attention to myself.

Fifty-plus entrepreneurs and professionals were assembled in a conference room that had been set like a classroom with long rows of tables and chairs facing the front. It was chilly, as most hotel conference rooms are, and I sipped hot coffee to stay warm.

After her brief welcome, Ursula dove straight in, "Let's start by writing down your limiting beliefs about sales."

Easy.

I am not qualified.

As I wrote down the words and reread them to myself, I was suddenly sad. Sad that it came to my mind so easily, and sad that it was true.

"Okay. Next, write down your limiting beliefs about money."

I am not worthy.

Damn. There it is again. Even after so much work. Should I be concerned?

I felt nauseous looking at these words on paper. I so desperately wanted this belief to change.

Then she had us write a new belief that encompassed both sales and money—a belief that we could repeat to ourselves.

I sat there for a few minutes, struggling.

Abby, why can't you write a new belief? This shouldn't be so hard.

I had so much resistance to money that I honestly couldn't write the word on my sheet nor say it out loud.

Is anyone else having as much trouble as I am? I looked around the room. *Nope . . . they are all head down and frantically writing their new belief. Why is this so hard for me?*

Ursula explained that she has studied NLP (neuro-linguistic programming) and believes that once we reframe the perception of our reality, we have the ability to influence and change it. This is how she was going to help us become more comfortable with sales and increase our numbers.

Hmmm . . . changing reality by replacing outdated thoughts with new empowering thoughts. Seems eerily similar to EFT.

At the morning break, a fellow Sales Camper approached.

"Is this you?" Jennifer asked, pointing at my LinkedIn profile on her phone.

"Yep," I replied with a proud smile.

"Why don't you mention Vivian Lou anywhere?"

Ouch. It was as if she had punched me in the stomach.

"Good question. I'm hesitant to mention Vivian Lou because I'm supposed to be looking for a full-time corporate job."

"Do you want another corporate job?" she probed gently.

"Hell no," I said with fierce conviction and a furrowed brow.

"Then change your profile. Go all in, girl." She said it like it was such an easy thing to do. So matter of fact. So sure that it was the right thing to do.

She was right, but I was still too scared. Too insecure. Too unworthy. The thought of updating my public profiles made me tremble.

NEW STEP

We spent that day and the next creating stretch goals, breaking our numbers into bite-sized pieces, creating plans, and taking intentional action toward achieving those numbers.

"Who's on your Top 20 Ideal Partner list, Abby?" Ursula asked as she approached my table.

"Local chiropractors, podiatrists, and shoe stores." My mouth suddenly felt dry.

In a very kind but inquisitive way, she asked, "Why do you want to play small, Abby?"

"I don't," I answered honestly.

"Then don't," she said with a knowing smile and casually moved on to the next Sales Camper.

I'd only spent a few hours with Ursula—at the free seminar and now at Sales Camp—but what I loved about her was how she could completely reframe my thinking with just a few simple words.

A few minutes later, she called attention to the front of the room and gave us instructions on how to cold call, walked us through examples, and asked us write our own scripts.

We knew what was coming. She had warned us the day prior. We were going to call our top prospects.

"Before we begin," she started, "I just have one question."

The room was silent.

"Abby, who's at the top of your call list?" She smiled at me from the front.

All eyes were on me.

Oh shit.

"Nordstrom." I gulped my cooled off coffee.

I just committed to a room full of people that I was going to cold call Nordstrom? Am I insane?

Ursula gave us thirty minutes to call our prospects.

I didn't know where to begin so I Googled "Nordstrom phone number" and found the customer service number.

I picked up my cell phone and dialed slowly.

Ring . . .

God, I hate cold calling!

"Hi," I started. "I'm looking for the women's shoe buying department."

"Sure," the woman on the other line replied. "I'll transfer you to corporate."

What? You're not going to blow me off? You're not going to apologize for not being able to help me?

Ring . . .

"Hi. I am looking to speak with the buyer in charge of women's shoe accessories," I said, trying not to sound nervous.

"Sure. I'll connect you with the assistant to the Executive Vice President and General Merchandise Manager for women's shoes," she said and then she transferred the call.

Wait. What? That's too high up the food chain! Too high! Please don't . . . My heart started to pound.

Ring . . .

Oh lord! Please don't answer. Please don't answer.

Ring . . .

Don't drop the phone, Abby. Why are your hands so sweaty? Gross!

"Hi. You've reached the voicemail of . . ."

Oh God! What do I say?

"Please leave a message, and I'll . . ."

Oh God! Check your notes, Abby. It's in your notes.

BEEP!

"Hi, my name is Abby Walker, and I'm the CEO of Vivian Lou," I read from my script.

Slow down, you sound too rehearsed . . .

"Imagine if all high-heel wearing Nordstrom customers purchased even just one more pair of heels every season because they now wear them four times longer without pain," I continued.

Almost done . . .

I read the script as naturally as I could, finishing with, "I look forward to connecting," before I hung up the call.

NEW STEP

OMG! You did it! You really did it!

My hands were shaking. I was out of breath. But I couldn't believe I did it!

I just cold called friggin' Nordstrom!

I was inspired. So I Googled the phone numbers for Zappos, DSW, and Zulily.

It got easier with every call. I never connected with a LIVE person, but I did leave some pretty amazing voicemails.

I am NOT playing small anymore!

Ten minutes later, as we were reconvening in the conference room, I received a call back from Nordstrom with the name, number, and email of the woman in charge of purchasing shoe accessories.

Make a call to Nordstrom and get a call back in ten minutes? Sure! Why not?

I left Sales Camp, dreaming bigger dreams and knowing that things didn't have to be as hard as they had seemed before this event. I mean, look at what I had just done in thirty minutes for heaven's sake.

But I still wasn't ready to update my LinkedIn profile or Facebook page.

That evening, I picked up the kiddos from daycare and camp and floated into the house. We arrived home just before Bill walked in the door.

He greeted the kids with a kiss on the head and walked over to give me a hug. I hadn't yet changed out of my clothes and was still wearing a favorite pair of heels—white patent-leather peep toes with yellow and green trim—when he asked about Sales Camp.

I told him about my amazing day, feeling myself expand with excitement with every word.

"That's great, Honey." And then he asked, "So how's the job search going?"

I winced. And stopped dead in my tracks.

"Good," I said, lying through my teeth. And Bill knew it. "But I'll do more tomorrow."

He looked at me sideways and headed upstairs to get changed.

I'll do more tomorrow . . . to find a job . . . and to use everything I just learned to grow Vivian Lou so I don't have to take that job!

I smiled to myself because Bill had just upped the ante, and I was determined to win.

A WANDER DOWN MEMORY LANE
YEAR 3 MONTH 4

It was now a beautiful but hot and humid Minnesota summer. The grass sparkled emerald green, flowers spilled over their pots, and mosquitos swarmed.

I had moved my working space from the three-season room because it was just too damn hot to sit out there and was now perched in the kitchen at the cooler granite countertops that I loved so much.

I really need to upgrade our bar stools, I thought to myself as I stretched my back. It was not the most comfortable place to work, but it was far better than melting in the three-season room or disappearing into the dungeon.

I opened my computer and started searching. Not for a job. But for a way to get Vivian Lou off the ground.

I had an amazing product. I had the guts and courage and desire to make it successful. I had the determination to no longer play small. But I still struggled with how to take Vivian Lou to the next level. I knew I needed to figure out why I couldn't write that new belief around money and sales at Sales Camp, or I'd be stuck.

"Hi, Greg." I sat down in the sun that was streaming onto the grey carpet of our bedroom floor. I was still meeting with Greg once a week. And although I wasn't 100 percent comfortable with EFT or tapping, I somehow always felt better after our conversations. Heck, I even ventured outside of the locked bathroom to take our calls from the bedroom.

Progress.

A WANDER DOWN MEMORY LANE

Inevitably, every phone call ended with me sitting in a pile of wet Kleenex, wiping away mascara streaks from my swollen eyes.

Seriously, Abby? Why can't you make it through a session without breaking down?

During our sessions, I'd often remember seemingly innocent, everyday non-events and wonder why Greg was so encouraged by them.

"These are popsicle memories," Greg would explain. "Every memory or thought is trying to tell you something. These memories may seem silly or unimportant or easily explainable, but they left a mark. We have to explore them and clear the blocked energy associated with them."

I still can't believe I haven't told Bill that Greg is an EFT practitioner and I'm tapping away blocked energy. I'm awful!

A few minutes into this session, I interrupted Greg. "I just remembered something, but it's so stupid."

"That's okay. What do you remember?" he prodded.

The details flashed before me like it happened just yesterday.

* * *

The summer before seventh grade, my parents purchased a house ten miles away from the house in which I grew up. It might as well have been two hundred miles away because I was going to a new school and since we hadn't yet moved into our new house, my mom drove us to school for the first few weeks.

I was sitting in the front seat of our blue, full-size Ford conversion van, and my sisters were singing in the back.

"Hey, Mom?" I asked, staring straight ahead. My heart was racing. My palms were sweating. And I couldn't turn to face her. I was so embarrassed to ask.

"Yes, Sweetie," she said, keeping her eyes on the road.

I paused wondering if I should continue.

Just ask. You NEED to ask!

NEW STEP

"Can I get a training bra?" No explanation. No details. Just a simple question. And a wince of embarrassment.

Being the new girl, I automatically felt out of place. To make matters worse, I was the only girl not wearing a training bra when changing into her gym uniform before gym class twice a week. An easy way to start fitting in was to wear a training bra.

"Oh, Honey," my mom said, "You're not big enough. You don't need one."

Doh. I was mortified. I slid down in the front seat hoping my younger sisters didn't hear this conversation. I couldn't even look at my mom as I opened the car door and ran off into school.

She was absolutely right. I wasn't big enough. And I concluded *I am not worthy of a training bra—or of fitting in.*

. . .

"Good work, Abby," Greg assured me as I finished wiping the mess of mascara off my face.

"Thanks, Greg. I feel so stupid that these memories affected me like this," I confessed.

"Please don't feel stupid," he said trying to console me. "We can't choose how or why certain events affect us. They just do. You're doing a great job identifying and addressing these things so you can move on."

"Thanks, Greg. Chat soon," I said and rushed off the phone to pick up the kiddos.

During our next session, I remembered another one.

"Go ahead," coaxed Greg.

I took a deep breath and let all of the details flood my mind.

. . .

I hated playing the piano, and I was never good at it. But my dad wanted me to play despite my lack of talent and interest. He told me that as soon as I learned how to play "Für Elise," I could quit. I should have made it my mission to learn that song and that song alone, but I didn't dare question the protocol, my piano teacher, or my dad.

Being a talentless, painfully shy, introverted kid, piano recitals were cruel and unusual punishment. Although I could perform my song without error at home, I froze whenever I played in front of people.

"Abby." The teacher called my name, and my second-grade self walked down the center aisle, in her light blue dress with white tights and black mary jane shoes, to the giant black grand piano that sat on an angle.

Plopping myself down on the cushioned bench, I placed my hands on the keys. I was breathing so fast that I'm surprised I didn't pass out. My fingers started to move.

Wrong key.

I started over.

Wrong key.

I kept going.

Wrong key.

I kept going.

Wrong key.

Wrong key.

Wrong key.

As soon as the last wrong note was played, I stood up and quickly walked back down the aisle, head hung low, staring at the ground, not making eye contact with anyone. I don't know if anyone clapped because all I could hear was the pounding of my heart.

I was mortified.

When I reached my seat, I looked sheepishly at my dad, hoping for a consoling smile or a "good try" or a "you'll do better next time."

But he never looked my way. He just stared straight ahead.

I don't know if he meant to dismiss me, but in that moment, I determined *I am not worthy of eye contact.*

NEW STEP

• • •

"Good, Abby. How do you feel?" Greg asked.

"Like a total fool, but surprisingly, a lot better," I admitted.

This EFT thing really works!

A few sessions later, I remembered another one.

"Please share," Greg encouraged.

I could feel the embarrassment flood my body before I even started.

• • •

I was in the fourth grade. Mr. Kraus's class. I loved his class because he kept candy in the top left drawer of the file cabinet behind his desk. Occasionally, he'd allow us to stand on a metal folding chair and choose a piece of candy, and I always grabbed the butterscotch.

I believe we were studying autobiographies, and as part of a project, he asked Mrs. Jacobson, my mom's friend and the mom of one of my friends, to trace the silhouettes of our faces, which would later hang in the hall and accompany our written profiles. Mrs. Jacobson set up an overhead projector and had us stand in front of the light so that she could trace our shadow onto black construction paper.

"I'm done, Abby," she chirped, and I turned to look at the tracing.

Oh no! Oh please no! She traced the spikes on the back of my head? Doesn't she know those aren't supposed to be there? And now they will be hanging in the hall for everyone to see! Oh nooooooo!

As the eldest of four girls under the age of nine, I understood why my mom didn't have much time or patience for hair. All four of us had bad haircuts, but why was mine always the worst? I was the sweet little girl with the God-awful haircut. People looked at me and said to themselves, "What was her mother thinking?" I know this because I said the same thing every time I looked in the mirror.

A WANDER DOWN MEMORY LANE

I was mortified.

But that was my haircut. And I decided, *I am not worthy of even a good bad haircut.*

...

"Again, great job, Abby. You feeling any better?" Greg asked.

"Ummm . . ." I wiped my nose and checked in with my body. "Yeah, I do feel better—you know, beside the puffy eyes and snot."

He laughed, "Yeah, it's just part of the process. But you're doing it. You're making great headway."

"Thanks, Greg. Chat next week . . ." I said and hurried back to my daily life, absolutely amazed at how these apparently small moments had taken such a toll on my self-worth.

In my weekly catch-up calls with my sisters, I brought some of these memories up to see if they had suffered from them at all.

"Do you remember those awful piano recitals?" I asked Lizzy, and we laughed about how bad they were.

"Do you remember when Mom used to drive us to school every morning?" I asked Amanda, and we laughed about how long the three younger kids had to sit in the car because they had to drop me off at middle school before going to elementary school, which started forty-five minutes later.

"Do you remember when Stephanie came over to the house, and said, 'I didn't know you had a brother,' pointing to a picture of me and one of my awful haircuts?" I asked Rachel, and we laughed.

All three of my sisters had similar experiences, and I marveled at how these things didn't affect them the way they affected me.

I don't know why these events had such a damaging impact on my self-worth and not theirs.

But I didn't waste time trying to understand why. I focused on what I needed to do to overcome it.

NEW STEP

At this point, it was harder to work on myself than it was to work on the business . . . but I was determined to make it happen.

I WILL feel worthy and deserving, God dammit.

STOP TO LISTEN
YEAR 3 MONTH 4

"Abby, it's time," Bill said gently one day after work in July.

His eyes were tired, evidence that the stress of financially supporting our family alone had taken a toll. He had graciously given me three months to make Vivian Lou profitable. And I failed.

I know. I know.

I looked at the ground, too embarrassed to make eye contact and too deflated to respond. I was going back to Corporate America. I was going back to living the good life.

Damn it.

After dropping off the kiddos the next morning, I returned home, sat down at the kitchen counter, booted up my laptop, and opened a new browser window. I begrudgingly searched Indeed.com.

What: Corporate Communications

Where: Minneapolis MN

I clicked "Find jobs."

A few dozen openings appeared. Two looked promising, and I applied.

I didn't want to find a job. I wanted to get Vivian Lou insoles in front of the women who needed them most. But sales were still slow. June closed with $3,000 in sales and July was shaping up to be an even slower month.

DING!

NEW STEP

An email from Zulily. They replied to my inquiry from Sales Camp and wanted to sell the insoles in the August 15 Fashion Emergency event and the August 31 Footwear Top Pics event.

YES! Maybe this is it? Maybe this *will be the thing that makes Vivian Lou profitable?*

I was so excited, relieved, and encouraged.

DING! Another email.

Vivian Lou Insolia® weight-shifting insoles were featured in *USA TODAY*'s travel blog as one of six things every female business traveler should pack.

AMAZING! Maybe this is it? Maybe this *will be the thing that makes Vivian Lou profitable?*

I was so incredibly grateful for these amazing opportunities, but I soon realized that they weren't enough to move the needle significantly.

Perhaps it's time to dust off the old foot spray. I bet if I sell the foot spray and the insoles as a bundle, then sales will take off. I'm going back to the foot spray.

I drafted an email to Dr. Paul and pushed the "send" button. I immediately got *that* feeling in my stomach. And I knew *that* feeling all too well. It's the feeling one gets when they rekindle a relationship with an ex-boyfriend despite their better judgment.

Rekindling a romance with the foot spray was wrong, but it was a good distraction. I knew what I was doing wasn't good for Vivian Lou or me.

So I Googled "how entrepreneurs stay focused."

One result caught my eye—an interview with Todd Herman.

I've heard of Todd! Marie Forleo featured him on MarieTV last year. And Amy Porterfield interviewed him just a few months ago.

I was intrigued by his background as a founder of a performance and research company that consults with pro and Olympic athletes on the psychology of winning. And now he was using those principles to help consult and coach entrepreneurs.

I listened to every podcast interview and read every piece of content.

"How to use an alter ego to achieve peak performance."

STOP TO LISTEN

"What to focus on when you're just starting out."

"How to finish what you've started."

"Why multi-tasking is not smart for entrepreneurs."

And then I stumbled across Todd's 2-minute-and-36-second "Got Grit?" video on YouTube.

I really don't like the word "grit," but I'll give it a listen.

"People don't quit on their business because it's hard. People quit because they thought it was going to be easy."

This shit is definitely not easy.

"When you play the game of business, you're confronted with risks, failed attempts, and people on the sidelines saying, "You have no experience in this area. Who do you think you are to think that you're going to be successful . . . ?"

They're not people on the sidelines. They're thoughts in my HEAD!

"And it's supposed to be that way. Why? Because it keeps the wannabe's, pretenders, and only dreamers off the field. They want to push the easy button. But then they look at their bank account and they don't see any results, they end up going to the next opportunity, or they say, 'The plan that someone sold me just doesn't work.'"

My bank account is empty. And yes, the foot spray has become my next opportunity.

"No, it's because *you* don't work."

Ouch.

I paused the video because tears streamed uncontrollably down my face until I could no longer see the screen. This statement struck a chord more deeply than anything I'd read or heard before. He was right. I didn't work. And it sucked. After I composed myself, I continued watching.

"This is a hard path. And you know what? It sets your mind right when you look at it that way. Hard is a story worth being told and listened to. Because on the other side of hard is the version of you that's exciting to me. And the best part is, you have no idea who that's going to be. And you're not supposed to."

I want to meet that version of me. I wiped away the tears dripping from my chin.

"The very nature of confronting challenges and obstacles and dragons you need to slay every single day is going to cause you to tap into resources and a part of your mental toughness you had no idea was even there. So get on with it. Not just for you, but for all those people watching you, hoping you can be a source of strength and power that they wished they had."

Let's do this, Abby. I sat up straight at the kitchen counter.

"But remember, the moment you begin to rise, arrows will come your way. And nine times out of ten, they'll be coming from your own bow. Shot by the goblins of fear, self-doubt, and insecurity, and they're taking dead aim at the beating heart of the very next big action you need to take today."

Goblins of fear, self-doubt, and insecurity. Check. Check. And check.

"But those little goblins aren't invincible. They'll retreat into the shadows the more you face them down, shine a light on them, and show a grander vision for where you are going."

I am doing this. The tears stopped and my chin tipped up.

"So the next time you hear that chatter of 'who do you think you are?', just grin, put on your hardhat, turn your back, and let them see the sticker that says, 'I got grit.'"

Damn, Skippy. It's no longer "if," it's "when."

I was on my feet at the kitchen counter, hands clenched at my sides.

Something inside me had changed. I was more determined than I had ever been in my entire life.

I listened to this video every single morning for the next few months. It had become my pre-game pump up song.

Game on, Abby.

STOP TO LISTEN

Todd,

    I'm sure you had an idea to whom you were speaking when you created that video, and I'm quite certain it wasn't Abby Walker—the middle-aged, middle-class mom who quit her middle-management job and was sitting at her kitchen counter in Minnesota trying to grow her floundering company instead of searching for a full-time job. What you said and how you said it struck a chord so deep that I cried (and still do) every time I watch it. Your message was my call to arms, and I became more determined than ever to figure out my shit. I owe you some Sprecker root beer!

BY THE WAY

YEAR 3 MONTH 5

"Hi, Abby?" an eager voice asked when I answered the phone one hot and humid early August morning. I still officed at the kitchen counter after dropping off the kiddos.

"Yes?" I replied inquisitively. I sat up straight and wondered who was calling.

"Congratulations! We'd love to bring you in for the next round of interviews," said the recruiting manager for a large financial planning company in Minneapolis.

"Wow!" I replied with fake enthusiasm. "That's great news!" I laid it on thick.

I *was* so incredibly grateful, but I wasn't at all looking forward to going back to Corporate America.

I was, however, looking forward to our August trip to Michigan, and I wasn't the only one!

Later that night, William excitedly asked, "Mom, how many more days until we go?" He'd been asking every day for a month.

"Only one more day!" I said with just as much excitement.

Every year, I take the kiddos to South Haven, Michigan, for two weeks in August. South Haven is my oasis, my Heaven on Earth. Soft, sandy beaches. Warm Lake Michigan water. Locally made ice cream. There is no better place to be in the summer, and there's no better view than watching your sun-kissed children frolic in the sand and water.

BY THE WAY

As I packed up the car the next day, I thought, *I wish Bill loved Michigan as much as I do! His Heaven on Earth is Summit County, Colorado, and he'd say there's no better view than watching your bundled-up children ski black diamonds and the terrain park. I guess opposites really do attract!*

Since I was driving the kiddos solo from Minneapolis to South Haven, Michigan, I decided to make a stop in Delafield, Wisconsin, and spend the night with my sister Amanda and her family.

"Oh by the way, Abby," my brother-in-law, Todd, started as we cracked open beers after the kiddos had gone to bed. "I heard this really inspiring woman Rachel Shechtman speak earlier this week. You should look her up." He had recently returned from a retailing conference and seemed really inspired. "She owns what sounds like a really neat concept store in New York City where she rotates themes and merchandise every few months. I bet your insoles would do great there."

Awesome!

"This store sounds really cool!" I smiled. "I really appreciate the recommendation!" I took a sip of beer and the conversation naturally changed to some other topic.

But that night before I went to bed, I Googled "Rachel Shechtman."

"Rachel Shechtman is a former brand consultant for Kraft, TOMS® shoes, and Lincoln, who created a retail concept that would serve as a matchmaker between brands and consumers, integrating strategies of marketing, merchandising, and business development. In 2011, she launched STORY, a space that has the point of view of a magazine, changes like a gallery, and sells things like a store."

Whoa. That really does look amazing!

I signed up for STORY's email list and then decided to focus on my family holiday. The kiddos, my parents, and I spent the next two weeks doing what we do best—playing in the sand and water!

When we returned to Minneapolis, it was back to the grind. The kiddos headed back to daycare and camp, and I continued to pursue the corporate job opportunity.

NEW STEP

On September 9, I felt compelled to work in my dungeon of an office. I sat down at my oversized white desk, scooted in my black office chair, and for some reason, checked the STORY website again.

I read about the current STORY collaboration with Donald Robertson and then I clicked on the Events page.

My heart stopped.

#PitchNight Returns to STORY

STORY goes in search of the next great thing with help from HSN®'s Mindy Grossman and *Good Morning America's* **Tory Johnson**

What's #PitchNight? Glad you asked. It's STORY's signature designer open call—a night where creatives of all disciplines have the opportunity to share a product and the story behind it with a panel hungry for the good stuff. Equal parts community night and opportunity of a lifetime, it offers anyone with a ready-for-market product 3-minutes with STORY founder, Rachel Shechtman. For this iteration, Rachel will be joined by two women who know the next big thing when they see it: Mindy Grossman, CEO of HSN® and Tory Johnson, contributor to Good Morning America.

OMG?! I have to be there. It's only six days away? Shit. Am I too late?

I immediately applied. And while my fingers flew across the keyboard, something inside me told me, *This is it. This. Is. It.*

I checked my phone every five minutes for the rest of the evening. Who am I kidding? It was more like every thirty seconds.

Any response? Damn. Nothing.

That night, I slept with my phone, just in case STORY called. And the next morning, I tried to play cool. I followed the normal routine, trying not to freak the kiddos out with my nerves.

At 9:59 a.m., DING.

BY THE WAY

From: Pitch Night <xxxxx@thisisstory.com>
To: Abby Walker
Date: September 9 at 9:59 a.m.
Subject: Pitch Night

Hi Abby,

This email verifies that we've received your RSVP for our upcoming Pitch Night on **Wednesday September 16** . . . *but you're not in yet!* We take our designer open call seriously, so in order to confirm your spot, we need to know you've got the goods!

In order to qualify, you must meet the below requirements:

[Detailed description of qualifications]

Thank you,
The STORY Team

I replied with all of the requested information at 10:07 a.m. At 11:03 a.m., DING.

From: Pitch Night <xxxxx@thisisstory.com>
To: Abby Walker
Date: Sept 9 at 11:03 a.m.

Abby,

Congratulations! You are 100% confirmed for Pitch Night.

Pitch Night will be held Wednesday September 16 from 6–9 p.m. at STORY, 144 10th Ave. (at 19th St.)

We look forward to seeing you soon!
The STORY Team

OMG! OMG! OMG!
    Inside, I was going wild—jumping for joy and screaming with delight. But on the outside, I sat stunned. I could hardly move to pick up my phone. My arm felt like it weighed a million pounds, and my fingers trembled.

NEW STEP

I called Bill. No answer.

Damn.

I called my mom. No answer.

Damn.

I called my dad. No answer.

Damn.

I called Amanda. *Thank you for answering!*

"OMG!" I screamed and burst into tears. "I was just accepted to Pitch Night."

"I am so excited for you, but why are you crying?" She sounded truly concerned.

"I have no idea, but I think my life is about to change. You have to tell Todd that I owe him big time."

OMG! Could this really be happening?!

I hung up with Amanda and booked my flight to New York City without even checking with Bill.

I am going. And nothing is stopping me.

Todd,

You took an interest in my "hobby" business and thought of me when you heard Rachel speak. You shared her STORY and after doing so, I truly began mine. This simple conversation was the launch pad of one amazing trajectory. Thank you SO MUCH!

aury lou

PITCHING FORWARD
YEAR 3 MONTH 5

It was 4:30 a.m. on Wednesday, August 19, when my alarm went off and I jumped out of bed.

It was early, but I wasn't tired. I showered, dressed, and finished packing at lightning speed.

Samples of the product. Check.

Folders with information and pricing. Check.

My nerves. Check.

I kissed Bill and the kiddos goodbye and headed to the airport. I was on my way to New York City to introduce Vivian Lou Insolia® weight-shifting insoles to STORY owner Rachel Shechtman, CEO of HSN® Mindy Grossman, and *Good Morning America's* Tory Johnson.

I landed at LaGuardia at 9:30 a.m. and caught a shuttle to the hotel, where I checked in and practiced my pitch.

So honored to be here . . .

Excited to introduce you to these insoles . . .

Forever change the way you wear high heels . . .

Ever so slightly rotate heel bone up and back for an equal distribution of weight between the front of the foot and the heel . . .

Stop your feet from slipping forward . . .

Unlike all other insoles on the market . . .

By 2 p.m., I was a ball of nerves and couldn't stay in the room any longer.

NEW STEP

I changed into my dress, slipped on my trusty black patent-leather heels, and struggled with how to wear my hair.

Up? Down? UGH!

Thirty minutes later, I sat with my hair in a ponytail in the back of my Uber driver's Toyota Prius, knowing I was way too early.

Overeager much?

"Please don't drop me off in front of the store. I am really early," I told the driver.

"How about here?" he asked, pulling up to the curb.

"Perfect! Thank you!"

He dropped me off in front of Star on 18, an old-school diner with metal booths and a counter with stools. I slipped inside.

"I'll have a tuna salad pita and a Coke. Thanks," I smiled at the waiter who had no idea that I wasn't at all hungry because I was so incredibly anxious.

I sat in the booth for close to two hours, trying to get my nerves under control. One minute, I was fine. The next, I wanted to head back to the hotel. I was a mess.

After paying the bill, I walked outside to see if anyone had started to line up and saw that a few people were gathered outside STORY. It was 4:30 p.m., and we were told to line up at 5 p.m.

I was still early, so I turned the corner, and as I walked down West 18th Street, my knees got weak. Leaning against a building, I pulled out my phone and started dialing.

He picked up almost before the first ring was over. He knew I was heading to New York and how nervous I was and had offered to help if necessary. "Greg, I need help."

Hot damn, it is necessary!

"No worries. Where are you right now?" he asked.

"Standing outside, leaning against a building. There are people walking past me on the sidewalk." I forced a smile at someone who looked up just as I said it.

"OK. So you probably don't want to tap . . ."

Hell no, I don't want to tap. I can barely do it in the privacy of my own home. There's no way I'm going to do it in public.

"Can you discreetly tap just below your collarbone and quietly repeat after me?" he coaxed.

"Yes."

I tried not to look like a total fool as I repeated the words he gave me and tapped.

When I started to feel better, I looked at the time.

Damn. It's 5:05 p.m.

"Greg, I gotta go. I'll text you when I'm done to let you know how it went. Thank you so much!"

I had no idea if that helped, but I swiftly walked up 18th Street and turned up 10th Avenue. Several people had already lined up and I followed suit. After a while, I turned to see how many people had joined the line. It was now around the corner.

My God! How many people are pitching tonight?

"I am so nervous," I said to the lady behind me when her deep brown eyes caught mine.

"Me, too," she replied with a kind smile.

We were instant friends. Helya Mohammadian, the brave, kind, cool and thirty-something founder of Slick Chicks, easy-to-remove underwear designed for women with physical constraints and women on-the-go. She, too, wore all black, and her long, dark hair cascaded down around her arms.

Shit! Maybe I should have worn my hair down.

The doors opened and thirty-four entrepreneurs walked inside to register. I was number sixteen. Helya was number seventeen.

"Hello and welcome," Rachel said, standing on a chair in the middle of the store. It was a 2,000-square-foot store with floor-to-ceiling windows on two walls. The floors were concrete-like and felt industrial, but the walls and fixtures were cheerful, bright, and colorful. The current STORY featured artwork and collaborations with famed artist Donald Robertson,

NEW STEP

and I LOVED it! There was so much energy from the artwork and the Pitch Night participants. It was a charged room!

Wearing a casual white button-down shirt and a long statement necklace, with her brown, wavy hair held back by a pair sunglasses that were perfectly perched on top of her head, Rachel introduced Tory Johnson and spoke a bit about Tory's new book *Shift for Good*.

"Here's how tonight will work," she explained in a kind yet commanding voice. "You were each assigned a number. That's the order in which you will pitch. My team will find you when it's your time to line up. You will each have three minutes." She paused before continuing in a business-like tone. "You will not get a commitment from anyone tonight. We will follow up with you if there is interest in your product. I think that's it." She started to step down off the chair. "Oh," she hesitated and quickly changed her demeanor, smiled, and stood back up. "Thank you all so much for being here. This is one of my favorite nights. Let's have some fun and good luck." She smiled encouragingly and stepped off the chair. She and Tory, who was wearing a casual black dress and Christian Louboutins, headed toward the back of the store to get ready.

A few minutes later, a confident, middle-aged, well-coiffed blonde woman entered the front door and was ushered to the back of the store. Mindy Grossman had arrived. She walked toward the white folding table set up just in front of a wall with six tall giraffes painted by Donald Robertson where Rachel and Tory were already sitting. There was another folding table set up along the window, and behind it sat four girls with computers and notebooks. Five other STORY associates milled around, helping the Pitch Nighters prepare their goods.

Pitch Night had officially begun.

Helya and I looked at each other with terror in our eyes.

We mingled with the other entrepreneurs and took turns supporting each other. I calmed her down when she was having a moment of panic. She calmed me down when I was freaking out.

"OMG! I honestly don't know if I can do this," I said taking quick shallow breaths.

PITCHING FORWARD

"You totally have this," Helya said. "You have a great product."

BJ Dowlen, the founder of BodyworksBall™, an award-winning, stress-relieving, muscle-relaxing massager, stood tall and confident among the rest of the group. Wearing a BodyworksBall™ branded black shirt and a bright smile, she chimed in when she saw us collectively melting down: "You guys are going to do just fine. Just be yourself. That's all."

"Abby?" an eager thirty-something gentleman holding a camera interrupted our counseling session.

"Yes," I turned toward him.

"We never took your picture. Can you grab some of your product and meet us outside?" He smiled kindly and nodded his head toward the door.

Seriously? You want to take my picture right now?

I walked outside and wrote my company name on a dry erase board. I held it up with a box of my insoles and tried to smile. When we were done with the pictures, I headed back in to find my new friend.

After about ninety minutes, I was called to line up.

I stood in line behind number fifteen and watched the panelists as number fourteen pitched. Rachel asked quite a few questions. Tory touched the products. And Mindy took notes.

OMG! I can't believe this is happening.

I took two pairs of insoles out of their boxes and placed them on a tray, trying to make them look fancy.

They're invisible insoles, Abby. They're never going to look fancy.

I tried not to pass out as I was next in line.

"You're going to do great," Helya whispered from behind me when it was my turn.

"Hi. I'm Abby Walker..."

About one minute into my three-minute pitch, Mindy took off one of her maroon Christian Louboutins that perfectly matched her maroon dress and maroon glasses and placed it on the table in front of me.

"Let's see what they can do," she said with a huge smile.

"Ummm... okay. But they are permanent placement insoles. Once they're in, they may not come out." I smiled back.

NEW STEP

"That's okay." She leaned forward in her chair as I searched for the correct-sized insole and watched carefully as I removed the liner and adhered it to the inside of her shoe. As soon as it was in, she grabbed the heel and put it on.

Before I knew it, Tory had taken off one of her Christian Louboutins and placed it in front of me. Same thing.

Mindy stood up and said something like, "I wish I would have had these last week! I wouldn't have had to take my heels off in the cab on the way home from *[some fancy sounding event that I had no idea what it was]*. These are great!"

OMG!

The only thing I could do was put my hands to my face in disbelief!

And just like that . . .

My three minutes were up.

I gathered my stuff and walked to the front of the store . . . shaking and trying to not burst into tears. I was so overjoyed and grateful that I was given this amazing opportunity to present to these iconic women, and that I made it through without looking like a complete fool!

Wow, Abby!

I stuck around to hear about Helya's pitch and connected with fellow Pitch Nighter, Erin Wexstten, founder of Oxalis Apothecary, who sells handcrafted, all-natural beauty products.

"How'd it go?" I excitedly asked Helya as she walked to the front of the store.

"I think it went well. I don't really know," she said. We grabbed some cans of Pabst Blue Ribbon beer and a bag of popcorn, which the STORY staff set out for the Pitch Nighters, and waited around to support Erin, who wasn't up for another ten minutes or so. Soon enough, Erin was called to wait in line. She stood confident and casual, wearing loose-fitting clothes that flowed off her slim build, very little makeup, and a perfectly tousled short brown hairstyle.

"Whew!" she said as she approached us after her pitch. "Glad that's over. Wanna grab a beer?"

PITCHING FORWARD

"Absolutely." A beer sounded like a great way to celebrate getting through that experience in one piece.

I didn't know where Pitch Night would lead, but I did know I was so incredibly proud of myself for stepping outside of my comfort zone.

> Rachel,
>
> You give entrepreneurs a voice and a platform from which to share our stories, and connect us "little guys" with the heavy hitters. Thank you for being such an amazing champion for small businesses. Pitch Night was a once-in-a-lifetime experience and opened some unbelievable doors. I will forever be grateful to you and your team!
>
> Avry Lou

SKIPPING WITH DELIGHT
YEAR 3 MONTH 6

"Please be interested. Please be interested," I silently wished every day following Pitch Night.

I so badly wanted Mindy Grossman to love Vivian Lou insoles and sell them on HSN®.

One week after Pitch Night, I found myself in the Subaru car dealership, getting a 60,000-mile checkup on our 2010 Forrester. When I walked into the service waiting area, I noticed how very quiet it was. Three people sat on two couches, staring at their phones, while they waited for their cars.

Maybe it's always quiet here this time of day?

I decided to sit at a tall bar table by the window.

R-I-N-GGGGGGGGG! R-I-N-GGGGGGGGG!!!

I usually kept my phone on vibrate, so I didn't realize it was my phone at first.

R-I-N-GGGGGGGGG!!!!!!

The volume was turned up. Way up.

The ring echoed through the dealership, and the three couch potatoes glared at me while I fumbled to find the phone in my Neverfull.

Why the hell is this bag called the Neverfull? It's always full. I've filled this bag with so much shit, I can never find what I need. Maybe they should call it the Neverfind?

I found my phone in time to see who was calling.

It was a 727 number.

SKIPPING WITH DELIGHT

727 is a Florida area code. HSN® is located in Florida. There's no way . . .
"Hello. This is Abby," I whispered.

"Hi Abby. It's Jane Dwyer with HSN®," she said in a very happy tone. "Mindy just dropped your insoles and your card on my desk and said I needed to give you a call."

OMG! Excitement bubbled up from my feet, through my stomach and into my throat. I tried my best not to scream right there in the car dealership.

"We'd love to take a look at your product. Can you send us samples?" she asked.

"Yes. Whatever you need," I responded, trying to keep my composure.

"Now don't get too excited, Abby," Jane warned. "There is a lot of work involved with getting a product approved through HSN®. Between quality assurance and legal, there could be a variety of reasons why this won't work out."

"I understand," I assured her.

But I KNOW it is going to work out.

It was subtle, but something had changed. I don't know if it was because I was now operating way outside of my comfort zone, but I was no longer scared. I was excited. Excited for all of it—the ups and the downs.

I had finally started to feel worthy. I had finally started to feel deserving. And I finally started to feel like my quest for the Red Shoes was taking off.

Five days later, I yelled, "Okay, guys! Wish me luck!"

"Good luck, Mommy! Good luck, Honey!" The voices of my three favorite people chimed happily in unison on Monday, September 28, as I threw on a trusty pair of black patent-leather heels and headed to my new corporate job as Senior Director, Internal Communications, at the large financial planning company.

I wasn't defeated or depressed because I knew I wouldn't be there long.

And, the way it so often does, the Universe confirmed my intuition later that day.

NEW STEP

I arrived home shortly after 5:30 p.m. and headed upstairs to change into my purple high-heel-printed pajama pants. Bill and the kiddos weren't home yet, so I quickly checked my Vivian Lou email and discovered an email from the buyer at STORY saying they wanted to place an order for the Home for the Holidays STORY.

"Yes! Yes! YES!" I screamed jumping up and down.

I closed August with $2,600 in online sales and was projected to close September with $2,800 in online sales. Despite the continually low numbers, I knew the tides were changing.

Thank you, Universe!

CLICKING BACK TO CORPORATE
YEAR 3 MONTH 7

I pulled into the underground heated parking garage five blocks from my building every morning around 8:45 a.m. after dropping the kiddos off at school and daycare.

Thank God for these heated garages! Who the hell wants to park outside in subzero weather?

I jumped into the elevators to the second floor SkyWay, a series of enclosed walkways that connected various buildings throughout Minneapolis. It was like walking in hamster tubes, and it took me exactly eight minutes in high heels to get from the parking garage to the office.

Thank God for these walkways. Who the hell wants to walk outside in subzero weather?

I scanned my badge and walked through the sliding glass security gate to the elevator lobby. It was a dark grey rather depressing elevator lobby. It was always crowded, but no one spoke, so I stood waiting for the next elevator with ten or more people while everyone looked down at their phones.

"Thirty-fourth floor, please," I said as I made my way to the back of the elevator.

I got off the elevator and walked to the far Northeast corner of the building to my corner cubicle. Normally, sitting in a cubicle would have really pissed me off, but in this building, offices were located in the middle of the floor so they didn't get any natural light or have any windows.

How depressing! I thought as I glanced at the offices.

NEW STEP

I pulled out my black, mesh desk chair, sat down at my angled cubicle desk, and looked out the floor-to-ceiling windows.

It was nice and sunny and private. But not private enough.

One week after starting at my new job, I received an email saying that HSN® transitioned my product from the Health and Fitness team to the Shoes, Handbags, and Accessories team, and they wanted to schedule a call.

I grabbed my cell phone and headed to the nearest conference room for some privacy just in time for the call.

"Hi, Abby. This is Ilka. So nice to meet you over the phone."

"Hi, Ilka." I tried to sound professional, yet talk softly so that no one would hear me. Cell phone reception in the conference room was not good, and I could only make out every other word.

Shit.

And so it went for the next two months, juggling a new job and an incredible opportunity with HSN®.

Job:
"Abby, we've scheduled you to meet with two new people every day for the next four weeks so that you can get to know the key players," my boss said.

"Great! I can't wait," I replied.

HSN®:
"Abby, can you send samples of the insoles to Sally in our Quality Assurance department? We need them as soon as possible," Ilka said.

"Absolutely! They'll go out tomorrow," I assured her.

Job:
"Abby, can you draft an all-employee note from the President of this business line?" asked my boss.

"Sure, but I've not yet met him. What are his priorities and do you have any tips on how to write in his voice?" I asked and took copious notes.

HSN®:
"Abby, you will need to register for Dunn & Bradstreet before we can move forward at HSN®," said Ilka.
"Sure. I'll get right on that," and I registered for a DUNS number through D&B.

Job:
"Abby, can you help us revamp the review and approval process for the customer-facing videos for this business line?" asked one of my employees.
"Sure! Can you give me some background on the business and how it's been done in the past?" I asked.

HSN®:
"Abby, we'd like to sell your insoles in a two-pair bundle," said Bianca, the buyer at HSN®. "Can we offer a two-pair bundle for $19.95?"
"Sounds good to me!" I confirmed, not knowing whether or not that would be profitable.

Job:
"Abby, you're taking the lead on one presentation and a panel at this conference," announced my boss at our weekly staff meeting. "Can you script the introductory remarks for the president of this business line and prep the five panelists, as well as create the presentation and talking points for the president of this other business line?"
"No problem," I replied with a smile on my face. "Can you run through that one more time?"

HSN®:

"Abby, we need to get official approval from Insolia® and the American Podiatric Medical Association before we can move forward at HSN®," said Sally with QA at HSN®.

"Sure," I replied. "I'll get you whatever you need." And then I called up Brian and Michael at Insolia® and asked them to help me gather the documentation.

Job:

"Abby, you need to write the Thanksgiving notes for four executives congratulating their teams on their accomplishments this year," said my boss.

"I'll get right on that," I said. "But whom do I ask for a list of accomplishments? I've only been here six weeks and don't even know the business yet."

HSN®:

"Abby, if approved, we'd love to launch your product around Easter as that's our biggest shoe buying season," Ilka emailed.

"Awesome," I responded. "Sounds like a great plan."

It was nuts. Why I wasn't freaking out was beyond me. I was on autopilot, blocking and tackling things as they came my way.

And just for good measure, Bill decided to throw one more thing my way one evening after he and the kiddos got home.

"Hey, Abby, we need to talk," he said, with a glimmer in his eye as he casually walked into the kitchen and leaned against the counter.

What is he up to?

"Yeah? What's up?" I asked, as I started plating dinner and cutting up the kiddos' food.

"Do you have any interest in moving to Rhode Island?" he inquired with a smirk.

What!?! I just started this new job eight weeks ago and now you're asking if I want to move halfway across the country?

"Sure!" I said. "As long as you don't expect me to find another new job." I winked.

Later that night, Bill and I lounged on the couch and talked in detail about the four companies that were heavily recruiting him. There was a good chance we would be moving in the near future, but where was anyone's guess. By 8:30 p.m., I struggled to stay awake so I kissed him goodnight.

Can life get any crazier?

TRUDGING THROUGH DEBT
YEAR 3 MONTH 8

"Welcome to HSN®! We are excited to have you as a new Partner and are pleased to welcome you to the HSN® Partner Community."

As I read the email the morning of November 16, I tried my hardest not to jump up and down in my cubicle.

OMG! Awesome!

I had so much for which to be thankful—a healthy family, a steady income, an amazing business opportunity, and a great husband who recently accepted a new job in Milwaukee, Wisconsin.

Four days later, I received a note from Ilka, placing an order for 1,100 two-pair bundles to ship in January.

What happened to Easter? Who cares? I have the inventory!

Two days before Thanksgiving, the plans changed. Ilka's email read:

"We have an event called 'American Dreams.' We think this is the perfect show on which to launch the brand. The show is currently scheduled for Jan 4. Items would have to ship mid-December in order to make it on time to the warehouse. Please confirm that will work."

"That will work!" I replied back.

So exciting!

Despite all of the excitement and activity, online sales were still less than ideal.

I closed October with $1,200 in online sales, and I was projected to close November with $4,500 in online sales, (due in large part to an amazing mention on RealSimple.com)!

Unfortunately, that still wasn't enough to cover the credit card debt I had accumulated.

Sitting in the dungeon of an office while the kids slept upstairs and Bill watched yesterday's *The Daily Show* in the living room, I quietly opened my credit card statement. This month's statement carried the balance from the previous few months and also included charges from my visit to New York City. I knew it was going to be a lot.

As I pulled the statement out of the envelope, my stomach tightened and my mouth went dry.

I was scared. I was ashamed. I was now $15,115 in debt.

And I didn't dare tell Bill.

Despite this debt, things are about to change. I just know it.

MANIC MOVEMENT
YEAR 3 MONTH 9

"OMG, Josh!" I squealed through the phone when my fulfillment center operations manager answered his cell on December 2. "I have the official purchase order from HSN®!" I was standing in the conference room on the thirty-fourth floor at the office, and I didn't care who heard me. "I am so excited and so nervous!"

"Congrats!" he replied enthusiastically. I could hear his smile through the phone. "Forward it to us, and we'll get going on it right away. Don't be nervous, Abby. This is awesome!"

I had good reason to be nervous—I had no idea what I was doing. Not a freaking clue!

And just to prove it, twelve days later, I found out that I'd failed to tell Josh that I was selling a two-pair bundle on HSN®, so they packed 1,100 single boxes—not 1,100 two-pair bundles.

Shit.

I picked up my phone and dialed Josh as quietly as possible from my cubicle, and explained the dilemma.

"Abby, we're more than happy to unbox and repack, but doesn't HSN® want the two-pair bundle as a single unit?"

"What the hell does that mean?" I panicked.

"Is the HSN® warehouse going to pick and pack two boxes separately, or do they want the two boxes together—like in a bag?"

Fuck if I know!

MANIC MOVEMENT

"Ummmm . . . I don't know," I admitted. At this point, I was totally flying by the seat of my pants, and I desperately needed help. "Let me check and get back to you."

Shit! I am not going to screw this up! I was panicked, but determined.

It was December 16, and I had already missed the original ship date by one day. The conference room was no longer an option, as I was too upset to care about the volume of my voice. So I started making calls from the thirty-second floor conference room.

"Hi, Sally," I frantically called the QA Manager at HSN®. "I have a question for you."

More like fifty questions.

"Oh Abby," she said consolingly. "Did you not read the Vendor Manual?"

I don't read instructions. Do you think I'm going to read a five-hundred-page Vendor Manual?

"Nope. I'm so sorry, Sally!" I said, as my face got hot with embarrassment.

"No worries. Yes, we will need you to place the two boxes into a plastic bag. These two-pair bundles will now become separate units with their own UPC code based on size. You will need to send me new samples to approve before you ship to our warehouse."

"Okay. Thanks so much," I said, trying to keep the panic out of my voice.

"I'm also going to put you in touch with Diane who can help you with specific labeling requirements for the bags, the master cases, and the pallets."

Okay, good. Because I have no idea what I'm doing!

"Thank you, Sally." I hung up, took a deep breath, and shook my head.

It's going to be okay, Abby. One step at a time.

Over the next twenty-four hours, I purchased new UPC codes for the two-pair bundles, ordered specific HSN®-approved suffocation warning bags for the two-pair bundles, and asked my fulfillment center to assemble two boxes in each bag, print labels with the new two-pair specific UPC codes, and apply the UPC labels to each bag.

Talk about drinking from the fire hose! I was juggling this five-alarm fire with HSN® while trying to work a full-time job.

In an effort to calm my nerves, I scheduled a call with Greg. Because I wouldn't dare tap at the office, I had to talk after the kiddos went to bed. But there was a slight problem: I still hadn't told Bill that Greg was an EFT practitioner.

I usually announced, "I'm going to take the call in the basement, but please don't come in the office, okay?"

On this particular chilly December night, though, I knew I was going to cry due to the massive amount of stress, and I didn't want Bill to think my "business coach" was okay with me bawling my eyes out.

"I'm going to take the call with Greg in the car tonight, okay?" It was more of a statement than a question, and he nodded in my direction to say it was okay.

I started the car and reversed out of the garage so I could sit in the driveway and blast the heat.

What am I doing? This is ridiculous! Bill must think I've either started a new gig as a phone sex operator or am having an affair!

"Hey, Greg," I said, "I can't do this tonight. I have to go inside and tell Bill about EFT."

"Oh," he replied surprised. "You still haven't told him?"

"No," I said embarrassed. "I haven't."

"Before you go, Abby," Greg encouraged, "let's very quickly clear some of this guilty energy so you can have a successful conversation with Bill."

I pulled the car back into the garage and found Bill in our dungeon of an office on his computer.

"Hey," I interrupted. "Can I talk to you?"

Turning to look at me, he said, "Yes, what's going on?"

"Greg's not my business coach," I announced.

"Ummm . . . okay," he replied curiously.

"He's my EFT practitioner," I confessed.

"Your what?"

Through guilty tears and a bit of embarrassment, I explained what little I knew about EFT and detailed my self-limiting beliefs and how, with Greg's help, I'd been able to move beyond them.

When he finally spoke, Bill said, "Well, I'm glad he's been able to help you, and I'm relieved you don't have a side job—or man." After a quick wink, he stood up to hug me and then turned his attention back to his computer.

"Hey," he said as I walked out of the room. "Just so you know, I saw you tapping—or whatever you call it—while you were on the phone with Greg a few weeks ago."

Totally mortified, I said, "OMG! Why didn't you say anything?"

"I don't know," he replied. "It was none of my business."

"OMG, Bill!" I laughed. "I can't believe you didn't ask me about it!"

Could we be more different? I thought as I walked up the stairs. *I would have interrupted his call and asked him right then and there what the hell he was doing!*

Two days after my EFT confession, the warehouse finished assembling the two-pair bundles per HSN® specifications and sent samples to Sally for final QA approval on December 18.

When I saw the email from Josh, confirming that the order had been assembled and boxed correctly, I collapsed into a pile on my desk. I was so incredibly relieved!

Thank GOD!

It was now three days past the required ship date, and we were in a holding pattern waiting for final approval from HSN®.

NEW STEP

Josh,

    You showed me tremendous patience, understanding, enthusiasm, and kindness. You could have very easily (and quite understandably) let me fumble this first HSN® order, but both you and Roxanne were in the trenches with me trying to figure it out. You worked overtime to make sure this order went out and took my calls whenever I needed your advice or input. You were an amazing business partner and friend.

Amy Lou

TRYING TO STAY GROUNDED
YEAR 3 MONTH 9

"You guys ready?" I asked the kiddos, putting the last of the snacks in my backpack. It was the morning of December 19, and we had arrived in New York the day before, which happened to be the same day the HSN® samples arrived in Florida.

Every December, for the past few years, we took the kiddos to Briar Cliff Manor, NY, to celebrate my niece's birthday and an early Christmas with Bill's side of the family.

We always scheduled a day in Manhattan to watch a show on Broadway, marvel at the Rockefeller Center tree, and eat pizza. There's nothing like NY pizza!

And this year was particularly exciting because we were going to see Vivian Lou insoles on the shelves of STORY!

"C'mon guys!" I pleaded, ignoring the urge to grab their hands and drag them. I couldn't get the family to move fast enough! Between Metro North and the subway, it took us ninety minutes to get to NYC's Chelsea neighborhood.

As I opened the door to STORY, all of the anxiety from Pitch Night came rushing back.

The security guard kindly smiled as we walked in, and one of the STORY team members joyfully welcomed us into the store. Dozens of customers casually browsed the thousands of unique items showcased beautifully throughout the store.

NEW STEP

After I calmed my nerves, the search was on. We started looking for the insoles in the store that was filled from floor to ceiling with the most amazing, unique items. Each section of the store was set up like an area in a house—a cozy living room with a fireplace burning, an orderly kitchen, a colorful kids room, and an industrial man cave—so that at least gave us some clue where to begin.

We started searching the shelves in the living room. William spotted them first. "Mom! Mom! These are yours!" he yelled at the top of his lungs.

I hurried to where he was standing, and there they were. Vivian Lou Insolia® weight-shifting insoles perched on a shelf next to the glowing fireplace.

Small, but mighty!

My heart nearly burst at the sight of the insoles displayed so beautifully.

Such an incredible honor to be featured among the other creative, extraordinary, and inspiring products featured here.

It was hard to peel myself away from them, but Bill and the kiddos wanted to check out the rest of the store. We visited every corner and looked at every shelf, found a few items to purchase, and headed back to look at "my" shelf.

And there she was . . . standing right in front of my insoles, rearranging merchandise on the shelf. When she gracefully took a step back to assess her work, I took a deep breath and approached. "Hi, Rachel. It's Abby Walker with Vivian Lou," I reintroduced myself.

"Of course," she said. "Hi Abby!" and she opened her arms to give me a hug.

"People love the insoles!" She was so gracious as we chatted about the insoles and fellow Pitch Night attendees. She introduced Bill and me to her sister and her parents (who just happened to be at the store), and she gave the kiddos some temporary tattoos.

"So . . ." I started proudly. "The product is going to be on HSN® on January 4."

"WHAT!?! That's amazing!" She held her hand up for a high five, and I reached up to give her one. "I can't believe you're going on air that soon! Congrats!"

"Oh, I'm not going on air," I said confidently. "They want to introduce the product as part of some American Dreams show. I think it's a product roundup of sorts."

"That's odd." She wrinkled her nose.

What's odd?

Changing subjects, she asked, "Did you hear? We're going to keep the insoles for the next Story as well—our 'Feel Good' Story."

"Are you kidding me?" I exclaimed. "Thank you so much!"

This is too good to be true!

"Yeah, but I want to make sure your insoles stand out a bit more, so I made a sign for them—something to place alongside the insoles to help tell the product story."

And then she disappeared without saying anything else.

Where'd she go?

I assumed she was called away to tend to a customer, so we bought our items, put on our coats and hats, and left the store to brave the windy but sunny New York day.

Waiting for the light at 10th Avenue, I heard her voice: "Abby! Wait! Wait! I want to show you this sign."

Rachel was running down the street, waving the sign in her hand.

OMG! I'm so embarrassed! Did I miss some social clue that I was supposed to stay? Oops!

Laughing, we all headed back into the store so I could take some additional pictures of the insoles with this amazing little sign.

While this trip to STORY was much different than my first, it was no less magical!

Two days later, I sat with Edie, Papa, Bill's sister, Stacie, and brother-in-law, Mike, at the dark wood table in Stacie and Mike's kitchen. Drinking coffee and watching the kiddos and their cousins play with the toys they opened the previous night, we were all still in our pajamas since our flight didn't leave until later that afternoon. And then it happened.

DING. I looked at my phone. It was an email from a casting specialist at HSN®. I was cc'd on an email to the buying team.

From: XXXX, Kaitlyn
To: XXX, Kaitlyn; XXX, Ilka
Cc: XXX, Erika; XXXX, Bianca
Sent: Monday, December 21 at 10:01 AM
Subject: RE:
Importance: High

Hi –

Just following up on the below—did you get the on air guest agreement from Abby? We need to get the ball rolling on approving her since she airs on Jan 4.

Kaitlyn
Casting Specialist - On-Air Talent
HSN®, 1 HSN® Drive, St. Petersburg, FL 33729

Wait. What? My New Vendor Training is January 28, and I'm not supposed to go on air until Easter.

I disappeared from the kitchen table and headed upstairs to figure out what was going on.

I called Ilka. On vacation.

I called her boss. On vacation.

I called the casting specialist.

"Hello, Kaitlyn?" I started nervously. "This is Abby Walker, and I just saw your email. I think there's been a mistake. I'm not supposed to go on air until Easter. Isn't American Dreams a product roundup show?"

"Oh. No, Abby," she said, laughing a little. "You're absolutely supposed to be here! You're going to be on air during the 7 p.m. hour of the *Monday Night Show*. Have you not booked your flight yet?"

HOLY SHIT!

"Um, no I haven't booked a flight yet," I said, not truly grasping the situation, "but I can do that today."

"Sounds good," she replied. "Can you also get us your on-air guest agreement? We need it asap."

"Absolutely!" I confirmed.

I screamed as I ran downstairs.

"OMG! OMG, guys! OMG! I am supposed to be on air January 4. OMG!"

I couldn't catch my breath. I was half laughing, half hyperventilating. *What. The . . .*

"Calm down," Bill said with a look of intrigue. "What are you talking about?"

I replayed the phone conversation with Kaitlyn.

"This is awesome!" Bill said with excitement. Everyone around the table laughed and clapped in agreement.

Awesome? This is anything BUT awesome. I'm going to be ON AIR!

I sat there stunned, trying to process how this was going to happen.

Me? On LIVE television? Holy shit! There's no way I can do this. There's no fucking way.

"Forward me the email, Abby," Mike offered. "I'll print out the agreement so you can sign it, take a picture of it, and email it back to her right now."

"I'll start looking for flights," Bill offered.

But there was hope. My product hadn't been approved yet.

Maybe this whole going on national television thing will be delayed, I secretly hoped while Mike and Bill problem-solved for me.

STEPPING OUTSIDE MY COMFORT ZONE

YEAR 3 MONTH 9

On December 23, the insoles were approved by HSN® Quality Assurance, and on December 31, the product listing went LIVE on HSN.com.

Holy shit. I'm going on air, I thought as I slumped forward on my cubicle desk, resting my head on my arms and gulping for air.

Since embarking on the Vivian Lou journey, I frequently operated outside of my comfort zone. But this was a whole new level.

This is fucking nuts.

I physically lost my appetite, but a new hunger grew inside.

You asked for this, Abby. You received it. Now make the most of it.

I sat up at my cubicle desk and went back to work.

ON MY WAY
YEAR 3 MONTH 10

"How's Colorado?" I asked Bill the night of December 31, after telling him that the insoles were now available on HSN.com.

"Amazing! The snow is perfect." His voice oozed with happiness and relaxation.

My dad and Bill were in Colorado skiing. They planned this trip months ago, before Bill accepted a new job in Milwaukee and before I was scheduled to go on HSN®.

"Well, Happy New Year, Babe!" I said, quietly wishing he were home.

"You, too! I love you. I'll call you tomorrow," he said before hanging up.

I popped open a bottle of Veuve Cliquot, turned on New Year's Rockin' Eve, and held up my glass.

Here's to an amazing 2016!

The morning of January 1, I finished packing up the car and yelled to the kiddos, "Go potty [cough, cough] and grab your backpacks [cough, cough, cough]."

We were driving from Minnesota to Milwaukee so I could find us a place to live and register the kids for school before Bill started his new job on January 19. I had mixed emotions about moving back to Milwaukee. I couldn't wait for the kiddos to be closer to my parents, my sisters, and their families, but I wasn't sure I wanted to move back to the place where I had existed as that shy, awkward little girl. Regardless, I had to find a house before heading to Florida for the HSN® show.

"See anything you liked?" Bill asked when he called during one of his ski breaks the next day.

"I liked two of them [cough, cough, cough]," I said. "I sent you pictures and videos of the places. They should be in your email."

Bill and I had looked at houses to purchase, but hadn't found anything we liked; and to be quite honest, we weren't that thrilled about buying another place. In the nine years we'd been married, we had owned and sold ten properties. We were totally okay with renting something this time around.

"I really like that white one in Mequon," he said that night after he'd looked at the footage.

Really? Mequon? I swore I'd never move back there after I graduated high school. UGH! But he's right. It's the better house.

"Sounds good [cough, cough]. I'll take care of it tomorrow."

That night, I didn't sleep a wink. I don't know if it was because I was sick with an awful cough, or anxious about the move, or scared out of my mind about going on LIVE TV.

Despite no sleep, I got up early, kissed the kiddos goodbye, hugged my mom, and drove to Mequon to meet Neil who owned the house we were going to rent. I gave him the signed lease and the deposit before heading to the airport.

When I was all settled into my seat on the plane, the gentleman next to me asked, "Why are you headed to Tampa?"

"I'm going to be on HSN®," I replied hesitantly in a quiet voice.

"Oh really? Are you going to be on air?" His interest was piqued.

"Yes [cough, cough]," I grimaced.

"Wow! What are you selling?" He leaned over a bit.

"Insoles for high heels [cough]," I said quickly, not knowing how much detail I should provide.

"Tell me more . . ." he coaxed.

Oh shit! It suddenly hit me. *I have no idea what I'm going to say on air. I never wrote a script or practiced how to introduce the insoles. OMG, Abby!*

ON MY WAY

Between my freaking out, the coughing, and the turbulence, I struggled to get through my explanation.

"Well, good luck," he said with a hopeful smile as we deplaned. "Maybe my wife and I will tune in tomorrow night."

Oh, please don't.

I arrived in Tampa at 4 p.m. and the Hilton St. Petersburg Carillon Park shuttle drove me to St. Petersburg. I checked in, ordered a hamburger with blue cheese from room service, and practiced what I was going to say.

"Thank you so much for having me. I am so incredibly [cough, cough] honored to be here . . ."

"These insoles will forever change the way you [cough, cough, cough] wear high heels . . ."

"Designed by a podiatrist and [cough] engineered by a rocket scientist . . ."

"Ever so slightly rotate heel bone up and back . . ."

How am I going to do this? I can't make it through a sentence without coughing!

At 9 p.m., I went to bed, but I didn't sleep.

This is night number two without sleep. Great. How is tomorrow going to go well? I thought as I watched the hours click by.

STUMBLING AND MUMBLING
YEAR 3 MONTH 10

"Hi, Sharon. It's Abby. I'm so sorry, but I'm not going to be able to come to work today. I am really not feeling well [cough cough]." I was mostly telling the truth.

As a new employee in the throes of preparing for a large off-site conference, I couldn't take a vacation day, so I took a sick day. And honestly, I was sick . . . I had an awful cough. But I was also in St. Petersburg, Florida, prepping for my debut on HSN®.

"I'll take an omelet, a coke, and the check right away, please," I said to the waitress. I wasn't hungry, but I needed to get out of the room after lying awake and coughing all night.

I sat in an oversized green booth at the hotel restaurant and stared out over the patio as I repeated the script in my head. It was a sunny day, but I didn't dare sit outside for fear of getting sunburned before going on air.

After four bites, I paid the check and headed back to my room.

Damn. It's only 10 a.m.

I paced back and forth in front of the bed, rehearsing.

You just need to get through the introduction, and then you'll be okay. You got this, Abby.

At 11 a.m., I called Greg.

"I am so nervous. [cough, cough]," I blurted.

"You're going to do great, Abby. We'll clear this nervous energy," he said.

We chatted for an hour, and then I got ready to go.

STUMBLING AND MUMBLING

Insoles. Check.
Shoes for display. Check.
Dress and shoes. Check.

"To HSN®?" the young hotel shuttle driver asked eagerly as I stepped onto the bus at 12:30 p.m. Per my itinerary, the on-air guest training started at 1 p.m.

"Yes, please," I forced a smile.

"First time on air?" he smiled back.

"Can you tell?" I gulped.

"You look a little nervous, but you're going to do great," he said kindly.

I'm not so sure.

He drove onto the HSN® campus and after being cleared by security, did a quick U-turn into the studio parking lot, and pulled up to the rather plain looking entrance. I grabbed my suitcase, stepped off the shuttle bus, and walked up the sidewalk to a door marked "ON AIR TALENT."

Talent? We'll see about that!

As soon as I rang the bell, the door buzzed open and a woman greeted me as I walked in.

"Abby?" she smiled.

"Yes."

"Hi, I'm Erika." The tall, blonde, wavy-haired on-air guest coordinator reached out her hand to introduce herself. "I'm so glad you're here. Training started at 12:30 p.m."

"What? My itinerary said 1 p.m. [cough, cough]."

"I sent an updated itinerary last week. Maybe you missed it?" she asked kindly.

Oh geez!

I followed her up a flight of stairs and into a conference room. Eight people were already assembled around the table.

"Hi, Abby," the young, energetic guest trainer acknowledged me as I entered the room. I placed my suitcase along the wall, found an empty chair, and scooted up to a corner of the table next to her. She wore an

NEW STEP

HSN® branded polo shirt and her long brown wavy hair was pulled back in a ponytail. "Please introduce yourself and your product."

"Hi. I'm Abby Walker," I said with a shaky voice, "and I'm selling insoles for high heels."

OMG, Abby! You can't even introduce yourself to eight people without sounding like a goddamn goat? How the hell are you going to go on LIVE TV?

We spent the next two hours reviewing how to greet the hosts on air, how big to smile, where to look, how to hold the product, what to say, and what not to say.

I'm just going to try to not pass out, I thought as I tried to take it all in.

And then we were off to a studio tour and training. We walked down the stairs and were buzzed into a long hallway. The floors were an industrial gray and the white walls featured brightly colored images of women modeling HSN® goods. The hallway was lined with tables of varying lengths that showcased that day's items—pillows, cutting boards, bagged food, and jewelry. There were probably fifty tables in the hallway.

We rounded a corner to another short hallway and then walked through an open door and into a studio. It was a large open space with three huge cameras facing an empty white table. Bright lights shone down from above.

"Here, put this in," the trainer said as she handed me an earpiece.

I had no idea what I was doing. "Is this in right?"

She grabbed my arm and pulled me closer. "Looks right," she replied and then she clipped on a microphone.

"Okay, Abby, count to ten slowly," the voice said in my earpiece.

"One, two, three, four, five . . ."

"You're good. Okay, now look at Camera One. Camera Two. Camera Three."

I looked at the cameras as directed.

"Good. Listen for our direction when you're on air. We'll tell you what camera to look in. Are you planning on demonstrating how these go into shoes?"

"Yes?" I replied not knowing if that was the right answer.

SHIT! I didn't think about or prepare for a demonstration.

"Good," said the voice. "Let's practice."

I grabbed a pair of shoes from my suitcase and demonstrated how to put them in a pair of shoes.

"Okay. Place the shoe on the table when demonstrating so we can get a good shot," the voice in the earpiece directed. "If you hold the shoe in the air, it shakes too much."

Let me get this straight. I'm supposed to simultaneously remember all the details about my insoles, carry on a conversation with the host, take directions from a guy in my earpiece, find the correct camera, and do a demonstration while keeping the shoe on the table? What have I gotten myself into?

I was totally overwhelmed. Void of any emotion. In complete shock.

"All right! Training is over," said the trainer. "You guys did great! You have time to head back to the hotel before makeup."

Lady, if I leave, there is no way in hell I'm coming back.

It was 3 p.m., and I wasn't scheduled for makeup until 5 p.m.

"Where's staging?" I asked the two cheerful, young ladies at the front desk. "I was told to bring in some pairs of shoes to put on the table."

"Take a right at the end of the hallway," one said with a kind voice. "And then an immediate left. It will be on your left side."

I walked back down the long hallway past the lines of tables. As the huge double doors opened slowly into the staging area, I stepped in.

"Hi. I'm here to drop off some shoes [cough] for the *Monday Night Show* 'American Dreams' segment," I announced to three ladies who were busy putting clothes on mannequins.

"Okay. Let's find you a table. Hmmmm . . . How big of a table do you need?"

What?! I have no freaking clue!

"I just have a few pairs of shoes and my insoles, so not that big of a table, I guess."

"How's this?" she pointed to a four-foot wide table.

"Perfect!" I chirped, as if I knew what the hell I was saying.

NEW STEP

I have no idea if it's perfect. Or if it's an absolute disaster. I have no idea about anything right now.

I walked back to the lobby of the on-air studio and sat in a cold, oversized, faux-leather chair and watched the HSN® channel, trying to glean insight as to how to act on air.

"Abby," one of the young ladies from the front desk announced. "Your green room's ready."

"Great!" I said, dragging my suitcase behind me and following her to my room.

I took out my clothes and placed the suitcase in a free-standing wardrobe that was placed next to the huge mirror lit by bright round lights above the makeup counter. I changed into my dress and put on my special HSN® shoes, smiling at the memory of Vivian's face when I told her she could pick out the shoes I would wear on-air since I was selling "her" insoles. She'd walked directly up to these incredible Sam Edleman strappy sandals with colorful beads and white jewels.

"Really, Vivi? These?" I asked, not exactly sure why I gave her permission to pick out my shoes.

"Yes, these," she replied, taking the display shoe and trying it on. "They're beautiful."

At 5 p.m., I walked back down the long hallway to the salon to get my hair and makeup done.

"How do you want your hair?" the woman asked.

"I guess straight with a little bit of body in the back?" I responded unsure if that was a good look.

"Sounds good, and your makeup?"

"I have no idea!" I gasped. "I'll leave it up to you. Whatever you think would look best." I smiled at her in the mirror.

Forty-five minutes later, she spun me around in the chair to see my 'on air' look.

OMG!

I gasped and tried my best not to cry.

Holy shit! I can't go on air looking like this. I look like a goddamn clown.

"What do you think?" she asked.

"I'm afraid it's too much," I replied holding back the tears.

"Oh, Honey," she said as she stood behind me and placed both hands on my shoulders. "It will look just fine on TV. I promise."

Fine? FINE? When the fuck would this ever look fine?

I ran into Erika in the hall after my appointment. "OMG, Erika! I look like a clown."

She laughed out loud. "I promise you won't look like a clown on TV," she said as she ushered me into the host room where I was scheduled to meet with Adam Freeman, host of *The Monday Night Show* and the "American Dreams" segment.

"Abby?" Adam asked in his boyish British accent. He smiled kindly and looked me directly in the eye as he reached out to shake my hand. He wore a well-fitted blue blazer, a crisp lavender button down, and a blue and white polka dot pocket square. His dark hair was perfectly coiffed and his teeth sparkled a bright white.

"Hi, Adam. Nice to meet you." I smiled, wondering if this was the right-sized smile to use when I was on air.

"I'm so excited about your insoles. They're going to do really well tonight. So how are you going to introduce them?" he asked. He was enthusiastic, but not aggressive. He had a big personality, but was not at all cheesy.

I walked him through my rehearsed script.

"Perfect," he said. "See you in a bit. You're going to do great." He gave me a thumbs-up and flashed a genuine smile as I stood up to leave the room.

For some reason, I felt completely at ease in his presence. I felt like he was going to make sure everything was okay—that I was okay.

I headed back to the green room and was told to wait there until someone came to put on my microphone and secure my earpiece. I sat down in the chair and looked at myself in the mirror. I didn't see the teased hair or the overdone makeup—I saw fear. Despite my newfound trust in Adam, I was still terrified.

NEW STEP

Oh God! What am I doing here? Why am I doing this?

Thoughts of Bill and the kiddos flashed to mind.

My family. They are why you're here, Abby. So you can greet the kiddos as they walk in the door after school and not have to send them to after-school care. So you can ease Bill's stress as the main breadwinner. So you can be more present for your family. But what if I fail?

I took a chance and dialed Bill's number. "Hi, so glad you answered. I have a quick question for you," I blurted out when he answered his cell phone. He and my dad had just boarded a plane to Milwaukee from Colorado, and they were going to miss the show. "If I completely fail, I mean completely bomb, like throw up or trip or accidentally smash the cameras to the ground, will you still love me?"

"Ha ha ha! Of course!" I could hear his smile through the phone.

"Okay, good. Have a safe flight. I love you!"

I hung up and called my mom. "Hi, can you please put William on the phone?"

"Hi, Mom!" he said joyfully.

"Hi, Honey! If I totally mess up and embarrass myself tonight, will you still love me?"

"Yes," he replied, in his serious almost-seven-year-old voice.

"Thanks, Baby. I love you so much. Can you please put Vivi on the phone?" I asked.

"Hi, Mama!" she said, in her sweet four-year-old voice.

"Hi, Babe! If I don't do well when you're watching me on TV, will you still love me?"

"Yes," she said, not fully understanding what I was asking.

"Thanks, Sweetie. I love you so much."

"Okay," she said.

Nothing else matters. Let's do this, Abby.

I put my phone away and headed to the studio.

WOBBLING ON AIR

YEAR 3 MONTH 10

Brrrrrr . . . it's cold in here.

I felt a little shiver run through me as I walked into the dark studio at 6:55 p.m., squinting at the spotlights and trying to take in all of the activity around me.

Cameramen were positioning the cameras. Producers were bustling around. Set assistants were double-checking the table displays. And the other "American Dream's" guests gathered on two couches.

Amidst the hustle and bustle, I saw a man wearing all black and a headset waving me over.

"Sit here." He pointed to the end of the long, off-white couch. "We're going to tease the American Dreams segment."

What does that mean? What am I supposed to do?

I quickly tucked the bottom of my dress in behind my knees and sat down.

"Smile and wave, everyone," I heard through the earpiece. "Here we go in three—two—one . . ."

Oh shit! I thought as I started to wave and looked out of the corner of my eye to see what the others were doing.

"Coming up on tonight's *The Monday Night Show*, we have 'American Dreams' . . ." a male voice said, and I saw myself smiling and waving on a TV positioned directly under Camera One.

Am I smiling too big? Is this wave too cheesy? Is this really happening? OMG!

NEW STEP

As our host, Adam, walked swiftly into the studio, a pre-taped intro to *The Monday Night Show* played and people on set paced.

I glanced at Adam. He had his back turned to the camera and was doing what looked like some sort of pre-game pump up routine. He was looking at his cards and rocking his head from side to side as if stretching his neck.

Wow! Even HE gets nervous. Okay, I feel a bit better.

"And we're live in three—two—one . . ." said the man in my ear.

"Well, a very Happy New Year everybody . . ." Adam cheerfully started the show. After a few minutes, he walked over to the couch while explaining that "American Dreams" is a show for those who want to introduce a new product.

Oh no! Is it too late to run? I did not know where to look or what to do. I could feel and hear Adam getting closer. And closer. And soon he was standing right next to me. I sat stunned.

"I want to introduce you to a special person, the lovely Abby," Adam said kindly. "Are you ready, Abby?"

"I am," I replied calmly while every single cell in my body screamed, *You are NOT ready! You are NOT ready, Abby!*

I got up off the couch and followed him to a different area of the set where my shoes were nicely displayed on the table.

Oh good. It was the right-sized table.

Adam walked to the far side of the table, while I walked to the one closest to me and looked down to see Adam's show notes and cards.

Shit! I am in the wrong spot! I looked over at Adam—the consummate professional—and let out a little laugh.

"Oh, we're in the wrong spot," he said, trying to walk around the back of the table, but it was blocked by a couch.

"Let's switch," I said, laughing way too loud. We crossed in front of the table—me still laughing—and settled on our respective sides of the table.

Whew . . . okay! Some light laughter to start. This is good . . .

Adam introduced the product flawlessly and then tossed it to me smoothly: "Abby, tell me about your love affair with high heels."

This wasn't in my script? Oh no . . .

"Well, thank you, Adam. I am so honored to be here tonight. And yes, Adam, I am a true high heel lover. I wear high heels almost every . . ."

In my earpiece, I heard, "Camera Two, Abby. Camera Two."

Oh, shit. Where's Camera Two?

". . . day . . . uuuuhhhh . . ."

Oh no, what was I saying?

". . . of the . . . uuuuhhhh . . . year."

Fuck the cameras, I just have to get through my script.

"I know all too well the pain associated with wearing high heels. About a year and a half ago, I set out to find a solution to the pain that is caused by high heels."

Damn that sounded good.

"And Adam, I found it," I said and glanced his way.

Suddenly feeling more comfortable, I shared product details, talked through graphics on screen, and explained what women will experience when they adhere the insoles to their shoe.

"Abby, will you show us how to put these in?" Adam asked, pointing to the pair of shoes perched in the center of the table.

"Absolutely!" I replied a little too confidently. I grabbed an insole off the table and started, "You simply fold down the top tab like so . . ."

Oh no! I can't pull the tab down!

"Sorry . . ." I said. And I continued to describe how to place the insoles in the shoe. I pressed down lightly on the back of the insole as I had just described, and the stupid insole came off the shoe.

Dammit, Abby!

"Oops," I said. "It's difficult doing this backwards."

No, Abby. It's not difficult. You're just an idiot. Why didn't you practice this? I can't believe you didn't practice this!

"You're doing a great job, my darling," Adam said. "The pressure of LIVE television . . ."

NEW STEP

"I know," I replied. "So sorry, guys."

Just get the job done, Abby.

"Okay, there we go," and I continued with the demonstration.

Whew!

"Everyone here who has tried these is a big fan," Adam chimed in, "and we have a massive fan on the phone right now. It just so happens to be HSN®'s very own CEO, Mindy Grossman..."

WHAT!?!

"Smile into Camera Three, Abby," I heard in the earpiece.

Smile? My face muscles are shaking uncontrollably. My mouth is dryer than the Mojave desert. And I'm trying not to cry because Mindy Grossman called into the show. And you want me to smile!?

"I met Abby at STORY," Mindy started, "and when I saw the product, I said, 'I have to try these.' I put them immediately into my shoes, walked out with them that night, and the second I got back to HSN®, I said, 'We need these.'"

I turned to look wide-eyed at Adam in disbelief.

Is this for real?

"I live for these," Mindy continued. "Anyone who loves heels, anyone who loves shoes, anyone who wants to be able to be comfortable and fashionable, these are the best insoles I have ever tried."

Breathe. Just breathe.

I couldn't believe what I was hearing. I was so overwhelmed with excitement, joy, and awe that I literally had to tell myself to breathe. Not fainting had quickly become the priority.

"Thank you so much, Mindy," I said.

Mindy freaking Grossman just endorsed your insoles on LIVE national television and all you say is, 'Thank you so much, Mindy.' God, Abby. I really don't like you right now.

"And speaking of STORY," Adam continued. "It is owned by an amazing lady, Rachel Shechtman, who is also on the phone..."

"Are you kidding me? Oh my gosh," I gushed. "Hi, Rachel! How are you?"

WOBBLING ON AIR

My God, Abby! This isn't a casual, friendly call! You don't ask her how she's doing!

"Hi, Abby," Rachel said and shared how Vivian Lou Insolia® insoles had sold out during the holiday season.

Adam reached over to touch my arm.

Can he sense that I'm about to pass out?

"It did so well," Rachel continued, "that it's coming back in a couple of weeks."

Adam clapped while I tried to breathe. I started go numb and it felt like I was swaying in my shoes.

Keep it together, Abby. You got this.

"Everyone loves these, so scoop them up while you can," Rachel finished.

At that, Adam took over. "Rachel, thank you so much. I know that means the world to—" and he turned to point at me when he was interrupted.

"I know some people have shoe trees for all of their shoes," Mindy jumped in, "but I have these for all of my shoes." And she laughed.

Adam shook his head and laughed with her. "What an endorsement!"

"Oh my gosh," is all I said. "Thank you so much for calling in." I put my hand on my heart and looked down at the floor.

Please don't pass out. PLEASE! I took a deep breath and got back into the game.

"Abby, walk us through the before and after graphic again, will you, please?" Adam coaxed.

"Absolutely," I replied. "This is one of my favorite images because it so clearly represents the benefits of wearing Insolia® . . ." and I described the pressure map that was on the screen.

"I suppose this is a dream product for every lady," Adam interjected as I finished sharing the details.

"Yes, it's perfect for every woman. Whether you are an eighteen-year-old going to your prom or an eighty-year-old dancing at your granddaughter's wedding, this product is beneficial for all of you . . ."

Dang, that was good, Abby.

"This product works for any shoe . . ." I went on. And on. And on.

Okay, stop talking, Abby. You're now mumbling.

"Because, uh, it's clear, um, and invisible, uh . . ."

ADAM! Save me! I looked over at him, pleading for him to help me stop.

"Abby," Adam finally interrupted. "I have some news for you."

"Yes," I said.

"It just sold out."

"Shut UP." I put my hands over my mouth and closed my eyes. I didn't know if I was more shocked that I had just sold out on HSN® or that I had just told Adam Freeman to "shut up."

"Oh my God," I said. "OH MY GOD." The words got louder and louder because when I cupped my hands over my mouth, the sound went directly into the microphone clipped to the top of my dress.

"I'm thrilled to present this to you, my darling," Adam said and reached over to grab my arm so that I didn't fall backward. "This is a *Monday Night Show* sell-out pin that you must wear when you come back . . . and you must come back."

"Absolutely! Will do. I'd love to!" I gushed and leaned in to give him a hug. "Thank you so so much."

"Oh my gosh. Oh, my gosh. That was phenomenal."

ABBY! STOP TALKING!

"Stay right there, Abby," I heard in the earpiece.

When they cut to a graphic, the voice said, "Now you can go," and I slipped behind the cameras.

I gathered up my shoes and high-fived a producer and two set assistants on my way back to the green room.

I did it!

Mindy,

Thank you for coming to STORY that night in September and taking an interest in "smaller" brands like mine. Your calling into the show and giving such an incredible endorsement was above and beyond. You are an inspiration to female corporate warriors and entrepreneurs alike. I am so incredibly thankful to have met you and for the tremendous opportunity to sell the insoles on HSN®.

Ary Lou

KICKING OFF MY SHOES
YEAR 3 MONTH 10

As soon as I got to the green room, it started.

   Ding.
   Great job, Abby! (from Edie)

   Ding.
   OMG! OMG! OMG! (from Amanda)

   Ding.
   Congratulations! (from Stacie and Mike)

   Ding.
   You were great! (from Larsen and Matt)

Wait! How did they know I was on air? I made both sides of the family swear not to tell anyone just in case I completely bombed.

   Ding.
   You were amazing! (from Cyndi and Tony)

   BILL! I bet Bill told them.
   I was too excited to care.

KICKING OFF MY SHOES

I so badly wanted to call Bill, but he was still on the plane. So I called my mom.

"AAAAAAAAAAHHHHHHHH!"

Amanda, Todd, Rachel, my mom, the kiddos, and I screamed on speaker phone for thirty seconds before my mom stopped to take a breath and said, "That was unbelievable!" Most of the family was gathered at my parent's condo for a viewing party.

I sat down on the hair-salon-style chair in the green room, still unable to process what had just happened. My entire body shook as I looked at *The Monday Night Show* pin in my palm.

Am I dreaming?

"You're hair and makeup looked great! That dress was perfect. The shoes Vivi picked were amazing! Can you believe Mindy and Rachel called into the show?!" My mom went on and on, and I did my best to listen.

But really, all I could do was laugh and say, "This is nuts!"

I collected my things, changed my clothes, and spoke with a few well-wishers in the HSN® lobby before grabbing the shuttle back to the hotel where I swiftly washed the clown makeup off my face and changed into my red, pink, and white heart-printed pajama pants.

I sat down and wrote thank you emails to everyone who helped me get through the day because I could not have done it without the help of dozens of people.

I am so incredibly grateful! I STILL can't believe this just happened! My body was radiating with excitement and gratitude.

By the time I crawled into bed, Bill and my dad had landed in Milwaukee and watched the show. Then the call came.

"You were amazing, Babe!" Bill said with a tired voice. "A few too many ums and ahs, but you were great!"

We chatted about the sequence of events and then laughed about how he had told our good friends about me being on HSN® even though I made him promise not to tell anyone.

NEW STEP

"I just didn't want to miss it in case your parents' DVR didn't work," he admitted. "I knew either Matt or Tony would record it and make it immediately available so I could watch it when we landed."

"Fair enough," I chuckled. We said goodnight, and then he passed the phone to my dad.

"Okay, start from the beginning," my dad prodded, wanting to know every detail of the day.

I gladly ran through the day's events—how I arrived late, how I had to wear an earpiece, and how I miraculously made it through the LIVE show without coughing!

I love talking to my dad about this! He's the only one who asks such detailed questions and wants to know the ins-and-outs of these types of experiences. Since I became a self-sufficient adult and got married, my dad has transitioned from a not-so-silent skeptic to my biggest cheerleader. Now that he no longer feels like my safety net, my dad is free to watch my life—and more specifically, this journey—unfold without any presumed responsibility.

"Just one more question," my dad said. "How much time did you spend with Adam prior to going on air?"

"We only spoke for three minutes."

"You're kidding me? He knew your product so well, and you were so comfortable. It was like you had spent the entire day prepping."

"I know! I honestly could not have done that without him. He made it so easy."

"He was awesome," my dad said.

Yes. Yes he was.

KICKING OFF MY SHOES

Adam,

    Your guidance, patience, and humor helped me through this absolutely amazing experience. I was so incredibly nervous, but after speaking with you, I was more excited than terrified. I lucked out having you as my host, and I apologize for telling you to "Shut up!" on national television. Ha!

Ally Lou

ONE FOOT IN, ONE FOOT OUT
YEAR 3 MONTH 10 – YEAR 4 MONTH 0

I walked up the stairs of our rented house in Mequon, thinking about how crazy life had been the last few weeks. There was that night on HSN® and then moving our family to Wisconsin. Our items had arrived the Friday before, and we'd spent the entire weekend unpacking. Our top priority was getting the kiddos settled into their rooms, but I stole a few hours to set up my new office.

I love this space! It's PERFECT! I thought to myself as I unpacked the boxes and dreamed of spending all of my days in that office growing Vivian Lou to the next level.

My new office was at the top of the stairs on the second story of our rented house. It was a small bedroom with a wall of south-facing windows that overlooked the half-acre backyard. Bright, airy, and refreshing, I'd decided to place my white, oversized desk in the middle of the room with my back against a sturdy wall.

And then I sat down. I loved how it felt to sit behind my desk, but I knew I couldn't sit for long. I had to unpack and iron an outfit for tomorrow morning.

I'm so glad my boss was able to coordinate my working from this advisor office in Brookfield. It's funny that they still don't know I'm living a double life.

After the kiddos hopped on the bus, I pulled out of the driveway and navigated the back roads from Mequon to Brookfield, Wisconsin. It took me exactly forty minutes to pull into the parking lot.

ONE FOOT IN, ONE FOOT OUT

"Hi, Abby. Welcome to the office," said the office manager. I followed him to the back of the office. "You'll be sitting here."

I suppressed my reaction as we walked up to "here"—the middle cubicle in a row of cubicles cobbled together in a dark hall between the back entrance to the office and three advisor offices. The cubicle to the left was used for storage, and the cubicle to the right was completely bare and empty.

I smiled at the office manager and reminded myself of how grateful I was for this job, as I was still struggling with slow Vivian Lou sales and wanted to at least pay off my credit card debt, which was now at $26,000, before stepping out of Corporate America.

I closed December with $2,400 in online sales; January with $1,100 in sales, and I was on track to close February with $1,400 in online sales. The payment from HSN® wasn't scheduled to be deposited for another few weeks.

Why can't I figure this out? I wondered day in and day out, as I sat in the little cubicle and tried to focus my mind on the work in front of me. Three weeks later, things started to look up

DING.

"Holy shit, Bill!" I whisper-screamed from my cubicle when he answered the phone on February 4. "I just got an email from HSN®, and they updated their purchases orders through May. Combined, that's more than $80,000 in revenue."

Enough to pay off my credit card! Holy shit!

The largest purchase order totaled more than $34,000. I printed off the four-page order at the office, stapled it together, and carried it with me *everywhere*. I gazed at it while I ate lunch at my cubicle. I kept it on the counter while I made dinner. I hugged it goodnight and placed it on my nightstand while I dreamed of making Vivian Lou a truly viable business. This was a game-changer.

I was invited back to HSN® on March 17 to present Vivian Lou Insolia® insoles on *The List*—a fashion focused segment with Amy Morrison. And again, the insoles sold out!

NEW STEP

YES!

While doing business with HSN® was so damn exciting, I needed to find a way to grow sales on VivianLou.com. When March only totaled $2,400 in online sales, I hired a renowned Google AdWords firm out of New York City to help me drive more traffic to my online store.

I have to figure this out!

STEPPING BACK TO CAMP
YEAR 4 MONTH 1

"There she is," Ursula said, smiling in my direction, as I tried to sneak into the back of the conference room. I was back for another round of Sales Camp.

Wearing another navy blue outfit, she stood in front of a new group of sixty or so entrepreneurs and small business owners looking to up their game.

I waved and found an open seat three rows from the back of the room.

Where's the coffee? I looked around the room as I hung my jacket on the back of the chair. That morning, I woke up at the ass-crack of dawn and drove almost six hours from Milwaukee to Minneapolis. I was excited, but a little jolt of caffeine would help.

Just like before, Ursula started with self-limiting beliefs.

"Let's start by writing down your limiting beliefs about sales."

Let's see what you got, Abby.

> I don't like bothering people.

Holy crap! This EFT stuff just may be working! 'I don't like bothering people' is a far less limiting belief than 'I am not qualified.' Way to go, Abby!

"Okay. Next, write down your limiting beliefs about money," Ursula coached.

> I will never be able to support my family doing what I love.

NEW STEP

WOW! No 'I am not worthy'? High five, girl!

"Now write down a new belief that encompasses both sales and money—a belief that you can repeat to yourself daily," Ursula encouraged.

This is the real test, Abby. Let's see just how far you've come.

> I have every opportunity to change women's lives and to live in prosperity.

Hot damn! I like it!

Ursula then moved on to making decisions and setting intentions.

"The word decision is Latin for 'cut off,'" Ursula began. "Inevitably, every one of us reaches the moment when we need to cut off all other options. Close the door. Go all in. Burn the backup plan."

Ironic, I thought to myself during the morning break. *I am "on vacation," yet sitting in a hotel just down the street from headquarters. I could stop in and see my team and my boss, but they are my backup plan! Pfff . . . I'll just stay right here and focus on Vivian Lou.*

That night, as I lay in bed at the Motel 6 down the street from the hotel, something bothered me. Something felt off.

I was ready to go all in, but something was holding me back.

I changed into my navy-blue polar-bear-printed fleece pajama pants and pulled down the dark green comforter to lay sideways across the bed on the crisp, white (hopefully clean) sheets.

After ten minutes of staring at the off-white popcorn ceilings, it hit me like a ton of bricks.

The understated, simple, discreet, and boring cardboard Vivian Lou insole packaging represented the old understated, unworthy, and undeserving Abby.

That's it! I sat straight up as a bolt of energy shot through my body. *That's TOTALLY it!*

I needed to upgrade my packaging.

To what?

STEPPING BACK TO CAMP

I stayed up most of the night brainstorming ideas, but nothing felt good.

"Why don't you call Mindy Grossman and Rachel Shechtman and get their perspectives?" Ursula asked me the next morning after I shared my epiphany.

"Why would they want to talk to me?" I asked sincerely.

And in true Ursula fashion, she replied, "Why wouldn't they want to talk to you?"

I drafted emails to both of them, asking for thirty minutes of their time. Mindy replied in thirteen minutes and Rachel replied only three hours later.

Dang it, Ursula. You're always right!

At the end of Sales Camp, Ursula told us about Synchronize, a ninety-day immersion program designed to help entrepreneurs make a quantum leap in their sales. The program cost $10,000, and I immediately felt torn.

I love working with Ursula, and although I've only met with her on three different occasions, the impact she's had on my business up to this point is unquestionable. But this is A LOT of money.

I felt sick to my stomach and my hands were sweaty. People were packing up to leave, and I paced back and forth in front of my table.

I just purchased a large quantity of insoles from Insolia® and the HSN® payments still haven't hit my bank account. I'm now $37,000 in debt, and there isn't enough room on my Vivian Lou credit card to pay for this!

But I knew this was something I had to do. So I walked to the back of the room to sign up for Synchronize and charged it to the card that I used to purchase the vivianlou.com domain name.

Hands shaking, I signed the paperwork.

I turned to walk back to my seat and tears started streaming down my face. They weren't tears of fear or sadness; they were tears of relief. And I was no longer sick to my stomach—even though I was now $10,000 deeper in debt. I probably should have asked Bill if it was okay to invest this kind of money, but he still didn't know how much debt I had accumulated. And I was still too ashamed to tell him. But at that moment, it didn't matter.

I know this is exactly what I am supposed to be doing. And I'm ready!
And I would find out soon that I was right!

WALKING ON AIR
YEAR 4 MONTH 1

I had already sold out twice on HSN® and was on my way back for a third time, appearing again on *The Monday Night Show* with Adam Freeman.

Why am I so nervous? I'm on with Adam tonight! I should be incredibly excited.

The pre-show routine was now familiar. I arrived to the studio way too early and walked down the long hallway to the staging area where I set up my shoes on a four-foot table. I headed to the green room and changed into the black dress with white piping that I borrowed from my sister Rachel and slipped on a brand-new pair of fun black pumps with a white rubber sole.

I love these "athletic pumps!"

After getting dressed, I walked down the long hall to the salon for my hair and makeup appointment. And as always, I left the room thinking I had on too much makeup. I headed back to the green room, and just before I left for the studio, I called Bill and the kiddos and asked, "If I completely screw up, will you still love me?" The answer, like always, was a resounding YES.

I love my little family! And I am so incredibly grateful that Bill continues to support me in this adventure despite it not making any money. One day, I'll be able to "pay" him back! I just know it!

Walking onto *The Monday Night Show* set, I visualized myself selling out again, but I quickly shook the thought out of my head.

NEW STEP

You're going to jinx yourself, Abby! Things are moving in the right direction and you don't want the tide to turn.

But the thought resurfaced when the producers cut to a replay of the first time I was on *The Monday Night Show* and told Adam to shut up.

Can I do it again? I thought as my mouth suddenly went dry.

"And we're LIVE," the voice said in my earpiece.

"Isn't it terrible, watching yourself?" Adam turned to me with a kind smile.

"It is," I said, laughing. "It's awful."

"Don't let me see this! Don't let me see this!" Adam said turning his head, pretending to be embarrassed and laughing.

Quickly changing subjects, he exclaimed, "Welcome back!" and reached his arms out to give me a hug.

I welcomed his hug and thanked him. "I'm honored to be back."

"Do you know how many people emailed me after the show, asking about this product?" Turning to the camera, he continued, "This was one of the fastest 'American Dreams' sellouts."

And we were off.

For the next ten minutes, we chatted about the insoles, he asked me questions, and I responded. While my product demonstration wasn't flawless, it was much better than the first time!

Whew!

"Let's recap the benefits," Adam said, winding down the segment as he talked through how the insoles are different from others on the market and made his final push to purchase.

And then he said it again.

"Sold out!" Adam yelled as he turned to me. I put my hands over my face in amazement and shook my head in disbelief. "Abby Walker for the third time!"

I heard Bob Circosta, television's first home shopping host and HSN® royalty, laughing off camera as I tried to catch my breath.

HOLY SHIT! I just sold out three times in a row on HSN®! HOLY SHIT!

"Now you've got to say it again to me," Adam prodded. "What did you say the first time?"

I put my hands on my chest as if manually making myself breathe, and laughed, "Shut up!"

"There we go!" Adam screamed with his arms in the air, and he leaned in to give me a hug. "Congratulations."

"Oh my God, Adam. Thank you so much," I whispered.

"You deserve this," he replied as he handed me another sellout pin.

"Thank you so so much, Adam."

What an incredible honor! If I can sell out three times in a row on HSN®, I know there has to be a bigger market for this product. I AM going to make this work, dammit!

"Bill, there has to be a way," I desperately pleaded a week later. "If I can sell out three times on HSN®, I know there is a market for this product. I just need time to figure it out."

We stood in the kitchen of our rented house one night after the kiddos were in bed. It wasn't nearly as nice as the kitchen in our Minneapolis house. Instead of fresh white, self-closing drawers and cabinets, we gazed at dated, chipped wood cabinets that I had painted bright white the day we moved in. Instead of shiny, black granite, we leaned against gray-and-white speckled countertops. And instead of travertine tiles, we stood on large, off-white linoleum squares. But it didn't matter, we were so thankful for this house.

"I know, Honey. I want you to figure it out, too," he confirmed. This wasn't the first time I begged to focus on Vivian Lou full-time since returning from Florida after my third sellout. "I'll give you three months."

What did he just say?

I looked up at Bill and stared him straight in the eye. "What?"

"I'll give you three months to focus on Vivian Lou," he said in all seriousness. "But if it's not making money by the end of three months, you have to get another job."

My body almost exploded with excitement. *I can't believe he just said this!*

NEW STEP

"Absolutely!" I said and leapt across the kitchen to give him a hug. "I am so excited!"

This is it, Abby. It's GO TIME.

The next morning, I called my boss to give my two weeks notice, and after hanging up the phone, I opened up my LinkedIn and Facebook profiles and updated my title to President and CEO of Vivian Lou.

It's time to start owning the role.

A GENTLE NUDGE
YEAR 4 MONTH 1

"Here you go." Ursula handed me a large hot Passion Tango tea from Starbucks as soon as I had climbed into the front seat of her off-white Lexus RX and buckled my seatbelt.

I had flown in from Milwaukee for the day for our one-on-one Quantum Sales meeting, which was part of the Synchronize program. It was a sunny, bright, spring Minnesota morning, and my flight landed late enough to miss the rush hour traffic.

We valet parked the car at Hotel Ivy in downtown Minneapolis and made our way through the lobby to the elevators, exiting on the third floor and walking directly to the boardroom.

"First, congratulations on your *third* HSN® sell out," she started as we both settled into our chairs. "Absolutely incredible!"

"I know. I still can't believe it."

"So how did your conversations with Mindy and Rachel go?" she asked as soon as we had both pulled out our pens and notepads.

"I am still blown away that both Mindy and Rachel took the time to speak with me," I replied. "Mindy was so complimentary of the product and loves that the insoles are invisible and don't take up room in the shoe. She thinks the small, brown cardboard box that I currently have mirrors those attributes."

"Interesting," Ursula noted.

NEW STEP

"We also talked about how she rarely buys shoes from brick-and-mortar stores anymore because she can get about anything she wants online from stores like Net-A-Porter."

"And what about Rachel?" Ursula prodded, leaning forward.

"Rachel was so incredibly insightful. We talked about the exclusive agreement with Insolia® and options to differentiate the insoles by color or other resin attributes so that it's slightly different for each distribution channel. But the most significant insight was our discussion around packaging. She confirmed that the current box gets lost in a retail space and that there isn't a lot of room for education—which is critical in helping consumers understand why my insoles are different from others on the market."

"All great points," Ursula agreed.

"Yes, I absolutely love Mindy's take on the box, but I've decided I need to change up the packaging."

"Great! With that decided, let's dive into the numbers."

Do we have to?

"If we must," I smiled at her.

This is why I signed up with Ursula—to get comfortable with my numbers. But it was the last thing I wanted to discuss.

"Why don't you open up your projections spreadsheet?" she started.

"I HATE looking at my numbers," I said, wrapping some jest around the truth.

God, Abby, you sound like a whiny six-year-old who doesn't want to eat her peas.

"Okay," she said, not giving in to my complaint. "Well, we're going to project out a $500,000 sales year."

I almost spit my tea all over the table and onto Ursula's beautiful, crisp white shirt.

"What?" I laughed.

"You're going to plan out a $500,000 year." She was dead serious.

"You're kidding, right?" I squirmed in my seat like a little kid.

"Nope." She smiled, and pulled out her laptop.

A GENTLE NUDGE

I sat in the oversized, dark leather boardroom chair for five minutes, staring at the blank spreadsheet while Ursula jotted some notes and answered some emails. I had no clue where to start. All I could think about was how sick I was to my stomach, how sweaty my palms were, and how embarrassed and ashamed I felt.

I had no idea how much I had sold. I had no idea how much it cost to get my product out the door. I had no idea how to project future sales. The only thing I knew was how much debt I had accumulated. And that number scared the hell out of me.

I hate money. The idea of money—both having it and not having it—makes me sick. I don't want to do this.

Ursula sensed my struggle. She walked around the long, mahogany table, put her hand on my shoulder, and sat down in the chair next to me.

"You can do this, Abby," she said. "I promise you."

She was no longer talking about the spreadsheet; she was talking about my absolute resistance to money. I don't know how she knew, but she did.

"Let's just start with what you know," she said.

I logged into Shopify to check my store's performance and started plugging in numbers.

Year to date, my online sales totaled just under $9,000.

I searched my emails and totaled up all of the past and projected HSN® purchase orders.

Year to date, HSN® purchase orders totaled $90,000.

"Wait. What? I'm just shy of $100,000?" I said excitedly. "OMG! Who knew!"

"See!" Ursula said cheerfully in her soothing, all-knowing voice. "You can totally do this."

For the next hour or so, I played with the spreadsheet, projecting online sales, HSN® purchase orders, and various wholesale orders. While most of these numbers were total bullshit, I realized that looking at numbers was more empowering than horrifying—and that maybe, just maybe, $500,000 in sales wasn't completely out of the realm of possibility.

"Okay," Ursula began when we sat down for lunch. "Now that you know you're going to make $500,000 in sales this year, where is it going to go?"

"Huh?" I raised my eyebrows.

"Abby, money loves a plan," she said. "What are you going to do with the money once you have it?"

"I am going to pay off my debt, and I am going to donate a portion of sales to Dress for Success—Twin Cities and Women's Bean Project in Denver," I said confidently.

"That's nice," she said, cutting her salmon. "But what are YOU going to do with the money YOU make . . . the money YOU bring home?"

Honestly, I've been so concerned about paying off my debt that I never truly envisioned myself bringing home money.

"Oh man," I sighed.

"You need to think about it, Abby, because money loves a plan."

Wait! I do have a plan! We have a plan! Of course! I know exactly where that money is going.

"Bill has always dreamed of owning rental properties. I don't know any other man who wants to retire so that he can fix broken toilets and mow lawns. But Bill does, and that's exactly where the money is going to go."

"I love it," Ursula said. "That's perfect!"

We chatted and laughed and brainstormed for the rest of the afternoon.

As she was driving me back to the airport, she assured me, "Abby, this is going to be great. You're going to be great. You just have to work at getting comfortable with your numbers."

And she was right. I did have work to do.

"Oh, one last thing," she said as I stepped out of the car. "It won't be long before you're sharing your story with others, and I cannot wait to read your bestselling book."

She winked and drove off.

I laughed at the thought of me sharing my story.

Who am I to share my story? No one wants to hear from me!

A GENTLE NUDGE

And I laughed even harder at the thought of me writing a book.

What the hell do I have to say—"I'm an entrepreneur who's had some tremendous luck, yet is still neck-deep in debt"?

It was totally illogical and completely irrational for me to think that I had a story worth telling, but as I buckled my seatbelt on the airplane that night, I started to wonder.

What if one day I do have a story worth telling?

> Ursula,
>
> While you helped me become comfortable with (and in fact, now love) looking at numbers, your impact stretches way beyond money, pricing, commas, and decimal points. You encouraged me to see things that I couldn't see. And you gently, yet repeatedly pushed me outside of my comfort zone. In those hard, early days, you reminded me of how far I had come in such a short time and celebrated my ability to make decisions quickly, take swift action, and manifest some pretty incredible opportunities. I now know I won't fail. This business may fail. New opportunities may fail. But I won't fail. You gave me the greatest gift you could give anyone—you taught me how to believe in myself. This belief is so liberating and incredibly empowering, and you held it for me until I was ready to hold it for myself.
>
> *Amy Lou*

MAKING STRIDES
YEAR 4 MONTH 2

"Hi, Greg!" I sat down on the floor in the sun with my Kleenex at the ready.

"How's it going?" he asked.

"It's going well!" I chirped and updated him on the previous week, including my meeting with Ursula. "It feels really good to have these occasional thoughts of worthiness and sporadic visions of being successful - especially because the HSN® payment finally came through and I just paid off my credit card," I said. "But I'm having a really hard time seeing myself making money. How sick is that? I'm a business owner who doesn't want to make money."

Greg laughed. "What comes up for you when you think about money?"

"Honestly, my lunch," I mused. "I have such resistance to money that I physically get sick to my stomach when I think about it. I don't want it. I don't want to think about it. I don't want to talk about it. I don't want to hold it in my hand. I don't like checking my bank accounts. I don't like projecting out sales. I don't like money."

There. I said it.

"Seriously, Greg," I continued. "I am more comfortable drowning in debt than I am seeing myself with a lot of money. The thought of having money freaks me out."

I shared with him that I grew up a very privileged kid in an upper-middle-class neighborhood. I swam at our country club during the summer. I went to tennis camp. I had a car to drive in high school.

MAKING STRIDES

My parents paid for me to go to college. And I was gifted a car upon graduation.

"Sure, I'm embarrassed about how well I had it growing up, but that isn't cause for me to have issues with money. Is it?" I wondered out loud.

"We'll get to the bottom of it," Greg assured me, and we got started.

After a few weeks, I grew increasingly frustrated with myself.

Damn it, Abby. What the hell is your problem?

To truly realize the projections Ursula and I had mapped out, I knew I had to free myself of these ridiculous blocks. Part of me was prepared to let go. The other part of me was desperately holding on—as if it were physically protecting me from something. I could almost feel the internal battle waging inside.

It wasn't long before very random popsicle memories started appearing during my sessions with Greg: The first one was that of me sitting in the front seat of a rusted out, beater car on a date. The second one had to do with me waiting for my high school boyfriend to pick me up after working long hours so that he could pay for his own clothes and gas. And finally, there was the one where I was looking at the multicolored leather jacket of a guy I later dated in college who still lived at home because he took out loans for school.

Holy shit! It suddenly made sense. *HOLY SHIT! That's it!*

The people I dated and the person I married are absolutely *nothing* like my dad.

Now, my dad isn't a bad guy, and I love him dearly. He's an incredibly successful civil litigator, absolutely hilarious in social settings, and has wicked dance moves. He knows all of the words to every pop song, is a history buff, and can make friends with the wall. And today, he is my biggest cheerleader—the first to call, the first to congratulate, the first to share the news!

But growing up with him wasn't easy for me. I was the oldest of four girls, and he was admittedly harder on me than any of the others despite my being the typical good girl. I didn't push boundaries. I didn't break rules. I didn't ask questions. I didn't have a voice or an opinion. Yet, he yelled.

NEW STEP

He slammed doors. He shoved furniture. He called me ungrateful. He demanded good grades and a high school letter. And he constantly threatened to revoke things—like car privileges and my college education. I did everything I could to make him proud—and if not proud, at least not angry.

Yet nothing I did was ever good enough. Every accomplishment was followed by a "but..."

She plays piano, but she's not very good.
She's good at tennis, but she avoids her forehand.
She gets good grades, but I wish she would get straight A's.
She's successfully completed six journalism internships by her junior year in college, but she should pursue a career that pays better.

"Holy shit, Greg," I said overcome with both relief and sadness. "It *finally* makes sense. My dad was the breadwinner and held the purse strings. And I'm terrified that if I make a lot of money, I will become my dad—the dad I knew growing up."

Armed with that insight and a box of Kleenex, Greg and I got to work releasing those beliefs.

I need to let go of this shit. And fast!

Dad,

Thank you so much for encouraging me to include this part of the story. Thank you for admitting that you were harder on me than the other girls, but that if you had a chance to do it all over again, you wouldn't change a thing... because neither would I. While growing up with you wasn't easy for me, I wouldn't be the person I am today without you. This is a rather significant "You have food in your teeth" moment—thank you for letting me hold the mirror. I am sure you didn't know that having high expectations would leave such a mark, much less cut so deeply. To be honest, neither did I. Please know that I love you—I always have and I always will!

avry lou

MAKING STRIDES

Greg,

    You graciously and patiently guided me through the toughest leg of my entrepreneurial journey—uncovering, acknowledging, and dealing with my deepest issues, fears, limiting beliefs, and demons. Who knew I was so messed up? Ha ha ha! You have led me up peaks and down valleys without judgment. You've been patient, kind, soothing, safe, and somehow knew all of the right words to say. Thank you from the bottom of my heart. You helped me find me and establish a new relationship with success, worthiness, and money, and for that I will forever be grateful.

Avry Lou

BOPPING BACK TO PITCH NIGHT
YEAR 4 MONTH 2

Between my work with Ursula and my work with Greg, I started to transition from resisting money to wanting money. The shift started slowly, but quickly gained momentum.

The best way to attract money will be to reposition Vivian Lou Insolia® insoles with new packaging AND new pricing, I resolved while walking the dog one early May afternoon.

Walking the dog had become my "safe zone." For twenty minutes every afternoon or early evening, I gave myself permission to go blank. I didn't worry about what was for dinner or stress about Vivian Lou or try to solve the latest scheduling dilemma. Liberty and I just walked. Some walks, I thought about nothing. Other walks, I dreamt up the perfect vacation. Yet other walks, I allowed some of the best ideas to appear. Ironically, I made some pretty important decisions (and still do) in twenty minutes while picking up shit and carrying it home.

This particular afternoon, I knew I needed to shake things up—if not for the insoles, then for me.

I am going to disrupt the aftermarket insole marketplace. Well, to be exact, Abby, it's the aftermarket insole marketplace—for high heels. I smirked at myself and then determined, *But I am going to disrupt it!*

As I rounded the corner toward our house, I picked up speed.

Disrupt. It's the word Sara Blakely used to describe how she built Spanx from a single-product company operating out of the bottom half of a duplex to a multibillion-dollar company.

BOPPING BACK TO PITCH NIGHT

I threw open the back door, headed upstairs to the office, and Googled: "Sara Blakely disrupt."

"The big secret behind disruption is not having any idea how it's supposed to be done."

Wow! I've gone from being scared to make money a few weeks ago to now quoting the youngest self-made female billionaire. Talk about a quantum shift. Well, one thing's for sure, I don't have any idea how it's supposed to be done.

So I talked about packaging with Michael Backler, president of Insolia®.

"I'm thinking about a really high-end, high-gloss, 4–6 page, 8.5x11 magazine or brochure," I explained. "The inside cover will feature a pair of high-end shoes with the insoles in the shoe. The insoles will be 'glued' to the page (to illustrate how they should go in the shoe)."

"Love this idea," he replied, "but I caution you on spending any big money on packaging."

Yeah, especially because I'm still not making any money.

Then I talked about pricing with Ursula.

"What about $77? What about $45? What about $29?" I asked.

"When you've landed on the right price, Abby," she consoled, "it will feel right."

It doesn't feel right yet.

I talked, but I had not yet made a decision.

The next day, I received an email from Rachel Shechtman, asking me to share the next Pitch Night information with fellow entrepreneurs.

Absolutely!

I sent the information to a few fellow Minnesota entrepreneurs. Two days later, I received an email from her team asking if I'd like to attend Pitch Night as a former Pitch Nighter and share my experience with other entrepreneurs.

Hell yes! I thought as I closed out my email and walked into the salon to get my eyebrows and lip waxed.

NEW STEP

"That is SO cool," my esthetician Mari started. "I love these kind of stories. You know I work part time at the Kit + Ace clothing store in the Third Ward right?"

"No I didn't," I said. "Wow, you're busy!"

"We host a speaker series where we invite local business owners, artists or experts into the store to share their story. I'd love to pass your name along to the store manager. You'd give a great presentation."

NO WAY! Ursula said this would happen less than ten days ago! What's it going to be, Abby?

As I lay on the massage table, anticipating the excruciating pain of her ripping the dried wax strip off my upper lip, I muttered, "Sure, I'd love to."

Attagirl!

I hated speaking to any group larger than three people, and my palms instantly started sweating at the thought of me sharing my story in front of people, but this was part of the new me. Pushing myself WAY outside of my comfort zone.

Two days later, I was on a plane to NYC as a Pitch Night alum. I stayed at the same motel and Ubered into the city just like before. While I wasn't completely freaked out, I was still a little nervous.

"You can drop me right here," I pointed to Lingo, a boutique on the North side of the 19th Street just west of 8th Ave. The window mannequin was dressed in an all black shirt with a really cool western-style necklace.

I wish I looked more chic.

I had forgotten my belt at home and was on a mission to find a belt before the event. I walked up the stairs to the robin-egg-blue door and tried to open it. Locked. So I rang the doorbell, and a little black dog ran to the door, followed by a petite lady.

"Hello," she said. "Come on in."

After sharing way too many details about my outfit, I ended my ramble with, "so I need a new belt."

"No, you don't," she replied. "Belts are awful unless they are statement belts. Do you see anyone around here wearing a belt?"

Nope.

"Just tuck your shirt in, and you'll be fine!" she said and waited for me to do as I was told. "See?"

It was just before 6 p.m., so I made my way to STORY.

"Hey, Abby! So good to see you," Jenny Shechtman, Rachel's sister and COO of STORY, waved as I walked into the store. Jenny resembled Rachel with her long brown hair and her kind, yet commanding presence. "Here, put on a name tag so people know who you are."

I mingled with fellow Minnesota entrepreneur Andrea Gribble who had been accepted to pitch her children's book *The Von Awesome Family in A Digital Daze*.

A few minutes later, Rachel stood in the middle of the store to announce the rules of the event—just like last time, except with no chair.

"And tonight we have various Pitch Night alums here, so feel free to ask these guys your questions," Rachel said as she ended her spiel. She went down the line introducing the alums.

"Oh, Abby! I didn't know you arrived," she said and walked over to give me a hug. She leaned in before letting go and whispered, "I want to introduce you to Adam after Pitch Night is over. Don't leave."

Adam Glassman, Creative Director for *O, The Oprah Magazine*™, happened to be a Pitch Night panelist that evening.

I stood behind the green ping-pong table set up along the back wall in the front section of the store for most of the night and met quite a new few folks, including fellow Pitch Night alum Heather Burkman, creator of the Go Comb; Emily Cunningham, co-founder of True Moringa; Karen Young, founder of Oui Shave; and Rebecca Ashby of The Pink Orange.

"So I'm thinking of changing up my packaging," I volunteered to the group. Everyone agreed that I needed something different.

I shared my idea about creating a magazine-like package. Most pages would feature lifestyle images and information about the insoles, and the actual insoles would be sticky-glued onto an image of a pair of shoes on one of the pages toward the back.

Everyone agreed that it was great in theory, but just a bit difficult to execute.

"You know the packaging show opens tomorrow, right?" said a fellow Pitch Nighter in passing, referring to LuxePack, an annual creative packaging show in NYC.

"No way!" I screamed. I immediately pulled out my phone, signed up to go, and pushed my flight back.

Bill won't care, right?

After three hours of chatting and sharing ideas, almost everyone had left the store, and I stood chatting with two folks from STORY when Rachel walked over.

"Abby, I'd love to introduce you to Adam."

I took a deep breath. *Just tuck your shirt in, and you'll be fine.*

I double-checked my shirt as I followed Rachel to the back of the store. It was quiet, and the energy wasn't as intense, but the buzz of Pitch Night still lingered in the air. I was nervous, but tried to play cool.

Adam stood tall behind the white folding table and wore dark jeans and a white button-down shirt under a blue sweater. He was chatting with someone on his team, and while Rachel and I waited, it hit me.

Pitch Night alums aren't allowed to pitch the same product twice. Is this considered a pitch if Pitch Night is officially over? Am I not allowed to talk about my insoles? Oh God! I should have clarified this with Rachel!

"Hi, Adam! So great to meet you," I started when Rachel introduced us.

"So nice to meet you," he replied. I glanced at Rachel with a "now what?" look on my face. She cupped her hands together in front of her stomach and pretended to push me forward in a motherly-like move. And then she stepped away.

I followed Adam as he walked toward the front of the store and shared the details of how Vivian Lou Insolia® insoles are different than any other insole on the market.

BOPPING BACK TO PITCH NIGHT

"Interesting," he replied. "I just featured some high heel insoles in the last issue of the magazine."

Great. Just great.

"Let's see them," he held out his hand.

I handed him the understated, cardboard box. And he curiously looked at it.

"I'm updating my packaging," I said, embarrassed, and looked sheepishly at the ground.

"Yeah, you definitely need to change this packaging," he confirmed. "You need something more sophisticated and something that will pop." Then he took the insoles out of the box. "These are interesting."

"Here," I said diving into my Neverfull and pulling out a bag that I had assembled earlier that night with ten boxes of various sized insoles. "Here are some samples. Feel free to have the ladies at your office test them out," I offered, probably a bit too eagerly.

We talked for the next few minutes and his assistant offered to take some pictures with my cell phone.

"Rachel, come here," he yelled. "You have to be in these, too."

How cool!

I didn't want to overstay my welcome, so I thanked Rachel for inviting me back and introducing me to Adam.

"I'm sure the insoles will be featured in the magazine," Rachel said as we headed toward the door.

"No way!" I quickly retorted. "He just featured another brand of high heel insoles in the magazine, and I don't have my new packaging figured out yet. Why would he feature Vivian Lou insoles?" I questioned.

"Why *wouldn't* he feature Vivian Lou insoles?" she replied with a smirk as she unlocked the front door and I slipped outside into the black night.

It was a warm NYC May night. I walked down the street and sat on the bench outside of Star on 18 while I waited for my Uber. I visualized Vivian Lou Insolia® insoles in a late summer issue of the *O, The Oprah Magazine*™, but I quickly shook the thought out of my head.

NEW STEP

You're going to jinx it, Abby.

I pulled out my phone to distract myself from the thought and there was an email from Katie, the Junior Store Director from Kit + Ace, inviting me in to chat about upcoming opportunities.

Wow! What a day!

THE PERFECT PACKAGING
YEAR 4 MONTH 2

The next morning, I packed up my things and Ubered to the LuxePack show at Pier 92.

I took the elevator up to Floor 2, and after registering, entered the exhibit space. It wasn't an excessively large show like a Las Vegas tradeshow, but the space was filled with unique packaging concepts.

Hmmm. I like that eye shadow package that is part booklet and part makeup container.

This is interesting. A box that slides out like a drawer.

Look at that sleek, limited-run Christian Louboutin box. Oh, wow!

While I found quite a few options, they were all either too complex or too expensive.

I wish they had something like this magazine idea I can see so clearly in my head.

But they didn't, so I walked out of the show feeling a bit frustrated and really hungry.

"I'll take three slices of cheese to go, please," I said to the man behind the counter at the pizza joint just down the street from Pier 92. No one needed to know that by 'to go,' I really meant 'to Wisconsin.'

I'll just put them in my carry-on and heat them up for dinner tonight. Totally gross, but Bill and the kiddos will love it!

As I zipped the three cheese slices into my red, hard-case carry-on suitcase, it struck me.

NEW STEP

Yes! Of course! Instead of a magazine with multiple pages, I'll make it a 'hard cover' two-page brochure. And red. It has to be RED!

And then the ideas started to flow.

It'll be like two FedEx envelopes stuck together and open like a book.

Instead of an envelope on one side, I'll create a window panel so people can see the insoles adhered to an image of a shoe.

On the backside of this image insert will be the instructions on how to adhere the insoles to the shoe.

As soon as I arrived at LaGuardia, I opened my browser and Googled "envelope manufacturers."

"Damn you, Boingo!" I cursed as I waited for my flight.

So many good ideas, yet such a bad connection. I'll just write them down until I get home.

Over the next few weeks, I spoke with several envelope and box manufacturers. Some on the East Coast and some on the West Coast. Inevitably, they'd send me prototypes of a box with a flap on the front and I'd sigh or grunt in frustration every time I saw one.

I don't want a box! They will get ruined in the mail!

So I kept Googling.

"Pulver Packaging. Short-run paperboard folding cartons made in Chicago."

Bingo!

Two weeks later, I screamed with excitement. "OMG, Vicki!" I exclaimed over the phone to Vicki Pulver of Pulver Packaging. "Thank you! Thank you! Thank you! This is exactly what I've been looking for! You nailed it!"

I hung up the phone and thought, *Okay, now I have the packaging. What do I want it to look like?* The only answer I had was that I wanted it to be red so I Googled, "Red packaging."

My eyes scanned the results for an image that grabbed my attention. Coke. McDonald's. Stella Artois. Lindor chocolate. Swiss Army. Spanx.

Wait! SPANX! Yes!

THE PERFECT PACKAGING

I studied every Spanx package. I read articles about why Sara Blakely chose red to stand out in a sea of gray packaging and why she chose illustrated women because she had a friend in graphic design and no one else had put illustrated women on their packaging before. I loved it! I loved all of it! I wanted to stand out in the shoe accessories section of a store just like she wanted to stand out in the hosiery section.

Unlike, Sara, however, I did not have a friend in graphic design.

But I did have Google. So I Googled "shoe illustrations" and scanned the results.

Nice. Hmmm. Interesting.

About three-quarters of the way down, I stumbled across the most amazing fashion illustration of five ladies. They had on a variety of casual, but upscale outfits and wore the most amazing shoes!

OMG! OMG! There it is. That's it!

I traced the image to a Melissa Corsari—a fashion illustrator out of Milan, Italy!

Oh man! I bet she's licensed this image to someone already, and I bet it will cost an arm and a leg to have her create a custom illustration for me. But what the hell?

From: Abby Walker
To: melissa.corsari
Date: Tue, May 24 at 9:51 AM
Subject: Bespoke artwork

Hi Melissa!

My name is Abby Walker, and I have a small company called Vivian Lou (www.vivianlou.com). I sell an insole that empowers women to wear high heels 4x longer without pain.

I am redoing my packaging and have spent quite a bit of time online looking for inspiration. I stumbled across your work . . . and absolutely LOVE your style and designs!

Do you do bespoke prints/drawings? If so, I'm curious as to how much one might cost.

NEW STEP

For reference, I'd love one similar to the attached image.

I look forward to hearing from you!

Thanks!

She replied within forty-five minutes. The cost was affordable, but she was in the middle of a large project and wouldn't be able to complete the drawing for a few weeks.

Poop! I don't have a few weeks! I'm going to take a chance on licensing the original illustration.

Hi Melissa!

Thank you so much for your quick responses!

Is there any chance I can purchase the rights to use your current image? I would crop it so that just the knees down will show on my package. Attached is a very, very rough mock up of the packaging (graphic not rendering correctly) . . . I have a designer on standby who will correct.

If you would allow me to purchase the rights to use the image, how much would that cost?

Thanks!
Abby

She replied within thirty minutes with a YES! And it was still within my budget.

YES! OMG! YES!

I ran downstairs to grab my credit card from my wallet, and raced back upstairs.

HURRY! Buy it before she changes her mind!

I purchased the image and immediately launched Canva to start drafting some ideas. (Mom: If you're reading this, Canva is a FREE online graphic design tool available to anyone with an Internet connection.)

THE PERFECT PACKAGING

I put together a rough mockup of my packaging. I knew it needed to call to women—rather, scream to women—from the store shelves and the computer screen so I crafted a variety of statements and landed on: "Wear high heels 4x longer without pain."

Perfect! Now women will know exactly what these amazing little insoles can do!

With the mockup done, I needed someone who could take my ideas and turn them into print-ready files.

No worries! I'll just create a job on UpWork. (Mom: If you're reading this, UpWork is a site where you can search for, hire and pay freelancers to help with specific jobs—in my case, graphic design!)

I posted a packaging design job, and received nine responses within twenty-four hours. I was drawn to the profile and portfolio of Christopher Budde, but given that my insoles were primarily geared toward women, I thought I should go with a female designer. Two weeks into the job, I knew I had made a mistake, and I should've trusted my gut. The lady I hired couldn't see my vision at all. She provided a dozen different options, but not one of them resembled the mockup I'd shared. I paid the lovely lady for her services and reached out to Chris.

Over the next few weeks, Chris and I worked together to finalize the packaging design and sent the artwork off to Vicki to be printed.

It's perfect!

I was so incredibly excited and proud of this new packaging.

Now THIS is O, The Oprah Magazine™ *worthy!* I thought to myself. Filled with overwhelming gratitude and excitement, I gazed out the window, knowing I had another big decision to make.

NEW STEP

Vicki,

You took an interest in my little project and brought my vision to life. You were incredibly patient, insightful, and responsive, and I absolutely love my packaging.

Amy Lou

Melissa,

I am so incredibly grateful that Google "introduced us." I fell in love with your work the second I laid eyes on it. Those shoes, and by extension, you, have become a critical component of the Vivian Lou brand. You are a tremendously talented illustrator, and I'm honored to showcase your amazing work.

Amy Lou

Chris,

I had no idea how complicated the first designs would become. You interpreted my ideas and read my chicken scratch flawlessly. Ha ha! You were and still are an incredibly responsive, collaborative, and patient design partner.

Amy Lou

COMING IN HOT

YEAR 4 MONTH 3

$29 or $49 or $69 or $99? What should I do?

I sat in one of the dark-red upholstered chairs my mom dropped off earlier that week. I loved these chairs; Bill did not.

Perfect! I'll just put them in MY office. One will be my new desk chair. The other will be a guest chair.

And that's where I sat, staring out over the backyard and struggling with how to price the insoles.

UGH! There's not much margin at $19.95 per pair. And I no longer want to compete with Dr. Scholls or Foot Petals.

A price increase was absolutely necessary, but I was so uncomfortable with the idea that I repeatedly had to convince myself of its necessity.

These insoles are not drugstore or Walmart insoles. They are permanent placement, scientifically developed, extensively tested insoles. They were not designed to cushion, gel, or pad forefoot pain. They were designed to prevent forefoot pain by shifting weight. And by doing so, they also straightened posture and significantly reduced strain on knees, hips, and back.

I flopped back in my dark red chair and rested my head against its tall back.

I don't want to price the insoles to be greedy. I want to price them so the consumer knows the value and will take notice.

I craved third-party confirmation.

Perhaps HSN® will have some insight and, plus, I really should inform them about the new packaging.

NEW STEP

A few days later, I was sitting in the same chair, chatting with the HSN® buying team over the phone. "Hi ladies! I wanted to chat with you about the upcoming packaging change and a potential price increase. I don't know quite yet where I am going to land with the new price, but I'm absolutely open to talking through any pricing suggestions or additional bundling options to make it work for HSN® and for your customers."

"Sounds good, Abby. We'd love to see prototypes of the new packaging when you have them and let us know when you have more information around pricing."

We talked for a few more minutes and then said our goodbyes.

Awesome! That went well!

I looked at the clock and smiled. *Time to go get the kids!*

I left to pick up the kiddos and headed back home to make an early dinner as William had baseball at 6 p.m. It was a warm, gorgeous May night—a perfect night for a baseball game! Bill was going to meet us there, so I hurried through the dirty dishes to get us to the game on time.

DING!

From: Michael Backler
To: Abby Walker
Date: Mon, May 16 at 5:33 PM
Subject: HSN

Hi Abby,

As you may recall, I am currently in China. I received a call today from Linda* at HSN®. She was quite upset at you (not me or HBN/Insolia®). And I am sure you can guess that it was about your new price. Linda kind of implied that you used exclusivity as a reason why you can raise your price. I hope this is not the case. For now, Linda has told me she has not said anything to Mindy. I told her I did not know any details of your plans for HSN®, but if I were you, I would be extremely concerned about losing your relationship with HSN®. We should talk when I get back on May 23.

Michael

COMING IN HOT

Michael A. Backler
President, HBN Shoe, LLC
Insolia® – Science For Shoes™
www.insolia.com

What is THIS?

I was so confused that I had to read it a few times to truly understand what happened.

Are you KIDDING ME?

I couldn't believe that Linda reached out to my manufacturer to complain about me and bitch about a new price that wasn't even decided yet.

ARE YOU KIDDING ME?

My blood pressure started to rise as I realized she deliberately went around my back.

How the hell did she get Michael's cell phone number? Why didn't she pick up the phone and call ME?

My blood started to boil.

HSN® doesn't have a contract with Insolia®. HSN® has a contract with ME. Was she trying to get me "in trouble" with my manufacturer?

My mind was racing, and I replayed the conversation I had with her team.

I haven't decided on a new price yet! I called her team today to give them a heads up and ask for their suggestions on pricing, for Christ's sake.

I walked upstairs into my office, as I didn't want the kiddos to sense this silent, but potent rage growing inside.

I can't believe she put words in my mouth. She wasn't even on the call! I NEVER would have thrown around exclusivity—especially because my exclusivity contract was EXPIRED! (Fuck! We have to draft a new contract!)

I paced in front of my office windows. I'd never been this angry before. Never. Ever.

I was ON FIRE!

ON.

FUCKING.

FIRE.

NEW STEP

"OMG, Bill, I honestly don't know what to do," I said. He was in the car on the way to William's baseball game, and by now I was walking in circles trying to calm myself down while the kiddos played with Legos in the living room.

"Well," he said, "You get William ready for baseball and drive the kiddos to the field. That's what you do. I'll meet you there."

Damn, why is he always so level-headed?

I rounded up the kiddos and off we went to the game. Vivian immediately ran to the playground, which sat just behind the baseball fields. William set off to unpack his gear and start practicing with his team. And I grabbed the chairs from the back of the car and headed to the field.

"Hi, Honey," Bill said as he unfolded one of the chairs next to me. "How was your day?"

"Uhhhhh," I said clearly irritated. "Do you not remember the conversation we just had?" I sat back in the chair, trying to focus on the game, but I couldn't. I stewed. I chewed my nails. I tapped my foot. I was doing everything in my power not to explode.

I had become a mama bear protecting her cub, and I was not going to let some higher-up at HSN® disrupt my relationship with my manufacturer.

"Honey," Bill finally spoke. "This is killing you. Go home and call Linda. She's probably not there, but leave her a voicemail."

On it.

I was out of my chair before he finished his last sentence. "Thank you." I quickly kissed him and headed for the car.

I raced home intending to call Linda, but I called Michael instead.

Ooops! He's in China. Shit. What time is it there?

Riiiiing.

"Hi, Abby," he answered his cell phone.

"Hi, Michael, I can't believe she called you!" I started. I didn't ask him what time it was. I didn't ask him how his trip was going. And I didn't ask him if now was a good time to talk.

"Yeah, she was pretty upset at you," he confirmed.

"How did she get your number?" I asked.

"I have no idea," he replied. "Apparently, she used to work at a large national foot store company that used to carry our Insolia® insoles. Of course I'm familiar with the store, but I don't remember ever talking to her."

"Was she trying to get me in trouble?" I asked.

"I don't know," he laughed, "but why would we scold you?"

And then it dawned on me. "Was she trying to purchase the insoles directly from you and bypass me?" I asked.

"Honestly, I don't know," he replied. "Maybe."

"OMG! I am SO mad!" I yelled. It was totally unprofessional, but at this point, I didn't care. Michael allowed me to vent, and then tried his best to calm me down.

"Abby, we are in your corner," he reassured me. "And we will update our exclusivity contract as soon as I get back."

"Thank you, Michael. I truly appreciate your support."

After hanging up with him, I searched my email for Linda's name, found her phone number, and dialed. I probably should have taken a few deep breaths or walked around the block or danced to Flo Rida's "My House" to blow off some steam before picking up the phone . . . but I didn't. I was on a mission.

Of course, no answer.

"Hi, Linda. This is Abby Walker with Vivian Lou. I understand you called Michael Backler from Insolia® today and informed him how upset you are with me regarding a potential price increase. First of all, it is a *potential* price increase. Nothing has been decided, and I told your team today that I welcomed their thoughts on what would be best for HSN®. Second, I understand you told Michael that I threw around my exclusive rights as the reason for a price increase. That is absolutely 100 percent false. And finally, if you have concerns with any matter regarding Vivian Lou, you call ME. You have a contract with ME, not with Insolia®. I am appalled, offended, and quite frankly extremely disappointed that you would go behind my back and call my manufacturer who just so happens to be in China on business this week. Please call me at your earliest convenience."

NEW STEP

I was shaking with anger and a million thoughts ran through my head.
Was I too harsh?
Was I not harsh enough?
Do you think she'll call me back?
She better call me back.
I am really disappointed in you.
I am so proud of you.
That was completely inappropriate.
That was absolutely justified.
Thank GOD I had a session with Greg the next day.

• • •

"Hi, Abby. How's it going?" he asked in his super laidback way.

There was no "Hi, Greg." No "How are you?" I just started in. "I am so pissed, Greg. You have to help . . ." and I told him the whole story.

We tapped away some anger, but it still lingered.

After playing phone tag for a few days, Linda and I finally connected, and she asked if we could start over with a clean slate. I'm not one to hold a grudge, but I wasn't sure I wanted to start over and debated whether or not to walk away from HSN®.

Damn, Abby. This is so unlike you.

In my anger, I had forgotten the hundreds of other wonderful interactions with HSN®, how truly helpful everyone at the organization had been and how incredibly thankful I was for the opportunity.

Michael and I chatted again when he returned from China.

"Abby, I'm not going to tell you how to run your business, but HSN® is your biggest sales channel right now. Are you sure walking away would be wise?"

"I know," I sighed.

As part of my Synchronize arrangement through Ursula, I also met with business and operations coach Rebekah Hall. And fortunately for me, my session with her was set for the following day. This couldn't have been more perfect.

· · ·

"Rebekah, I've got something I need help with asap . . ." I started.

"Shoot," replied Rebekah.

When I finished the story, she said, "I get it, Abby. I totally get it. And, no matter how small you are, never, ever let the big guys bully you. Ever. You have the power here, and it comes down to numbers."

That's right. I sat up straighter in my chair.

"Is there potential to grow with HSN®? And if yes," she continued, "let's think through some options. Can you create a different version of the insole for HSN®?"

"What do you mean?" I asked, leaning forward with curiosity.

"Look at Ninja blenders," she said. "They offer multiple versions of their blender at a variety of price points. The version that's sold on QVC may be a lower price point and have a slower motor speed. The version that's sold at Macy's may include special attachments. The version that's sold at Bed Bath & Beyond may come in an exclusive color."

Oh, this is what Rachel was talking about!

Rachel Shechtman had suggested this approach two months prior as a way to get into higher-end retailers, but it didn't fully click that I could use the same strategy with HSN® until Rebekah said it.

"OMG, Rebekah!" I screamed. "You're brilliant!"

I had no idea how to do this with the insoles, but I hung up with Rebekah determined to find a way.

I also determined that I no longer wanted advice from just anyone and everyone. I only wanted advice from the people who had MY best interest at heart—not just an interest in my business. So I stopped communicating with a few mentors, and I grew leery of contractors and vendors who offered to discount their rates at the slimmest chance I'd let them have

NEW STEP

a piece of the Vivian Lou pie. By now, I'd had at least five individuals approach me about partnership deals.

DING!

From: Nicole
To: Abby Walker
Tate: Fri, Jun 3 at 12:21 PM
Subject: Oprah Mag / Vivian Lou Credit / Sept

Hi Abby,

Happy Friday! We shot the attached Vivian Lou insoles in consideration for September, can you send credit info when you have a chance?

***Please fill out the below form exactly how it should appear on page.

Designer/Brand:
Material:
Any Special Features/ Descriptions we should know:
Retail Price:
Where To Buy: (Please include a DIRECT LINK if the items are available now and if not an E-commerce site that sells this item):
Confirm this item will be available on stands starting 08/09: (yes or no):
Dimensions (handbags only):

** Please note this does not guarantee your item will appear in *O, The Oprah Magazine*™

Thank you!

Nicole
Fashion Features Editor
O, The Oprah Magazine™
300 W 57th Street |36th floor
New York, NY 10019

COMING IN HOT

Holy poop! Holy Poop! HOLY POOP!

I jumped out of my dark red chair and skipped around my office.

Rachel was right! OMG! THIS IS SO AWESOME!!!

I sat back down to reread the email.

OMG, she wants a price!? I haven't decided on a price. Shit! I guess I'm deciding a price right now.

$29 per pair.

Oh no, did they photograph the product in the old packaging?

Nope. Nicole confirmed that they shot the insoles without the packaging.

Whew!

And per her email, the new price would be in print on August 9.

AWESOME!

Now I just had to complete the new packaging and refresh the website by August 9.

No worries!

Oh, and I still have to figure out what to do with HSN®.

> Rebekah,
>
> You talked me off the ledge, offered sage and rational advice, listened to my side of the story, and suggested solutions that made sense for me—not just my balance sheet. You are a phenomenal coach.
>
> *Avry Lou*

STEPPING ONTO THE STAGE
YEAR 4 MONTH 3

"How did it go?" Katie, the Kit + Ace Junior store manager asked.

I stopped by the store on June 10 on my way home from the airport after another HSN® appearance.

"It went well!" I replied. "I didn't sell out, but I beat sales projections by 20 percent."

"Awesome!" she replied. "So let's find you something to wear for June 23."

June 23 was the day I was sharing my story for the first time and presenting at Kit + Ace.

When the day finally arrived, Bill entered the front glass doors of the store calm and collected. He wore his black-rimmed glasses, blue pants, and a blue and white checked shirt. And although he'd been at the office all day, his clothes still looked pressed from the morning.

How does he do that?

He tipped his head up when he saw me standing at the back of the store, grabbed a bottle of water from the table, and approached.

"You ready?" he asked smiling.

"OMG, Bill" I was full of panic. "I am so nervous!"

"You're going to do great," he encouraged and put his hand up for a high-five.

"If I totally mess up, will you still love me?" I asked, meeting his high five weakly.

"Ha, Abby!" he laughed. "Of course." He squeezed my hand to affirm his words.

As Ursula predicted, I was about to share my story.

The back of the store had been converted to a "stage." A projector was set up in front of the changing rooms, and benches were pulled out from underneath tables facing the projector. I watched from the back as people entered the store looking for a place to sit on one of the benches. Wine was being poured, and I was handed a microphone.

Only twelve guests showed up, but that was twelve more than I wanted. Sure, I had presented on LIVE national television four times now, but I always had a host lead me through the discussion. I was now solo on stage.

My mouth went dry and my heart pounded in my chest.

You've got this, Abby.

"Hi," I began nervously. "Thank you so much for coming tonight. I'm honored to be here to share my story and offer a few insights I've learned along my entrepreneurial journey thus far."

So funny that I'm here sharing my story as an entrepreneur when I haven't paid myself yet and I'm once again in debt...

"My story actually starts here—in Milwaukee . . ." and I spoke for about twenty minutes or so.

Bill stood at the back, watching me with a gentle smile on his face. Whenever I fumbled, I just looked at him and then found my way back to what I needed to say.

"One of the most important lessons I've learned," I confessed as I wrapped up, "is that presentations like mine tonight, and webinars put on by gurus, and courses offered by so-called experts are only highlight reels. You rarely see the true struggle people endure. So if you have any questions about my journey, I'll answer them honestly—including the parts I wouldn't put on a highlight reel." I laughed. "I promise you, it hasn't always been pretty!"

A few folks asked questions. Others commented on my journey. And it felt good!

I can't believe I'm saying it, but this was actually fun! I thought as I handed the microphone back to one of the store associates.

"Congratulations, Babe," Bill said after the presentation. "A few too many ums and ahs, but you were great!"

Everyone had left the store except for one woman who lingered. She had asked a few questions during the presentation, volunteered that she had years of experience in the footwear industry, and offered to share a few of her contacts.

"Thanks for coming," I said, as she turned to look at me.

"I really think you're on to something here," she said. "I have a ton of ideas for you, and would love to talk more. Want to grab a drink?"

"Of course! I'd love to. Let me tell my husband I'll meet him at home."

Bill left to pick the kiddos up from my sister's house, and she and I headed across the street. It was a nice June evening, and we decided to sit outside at one of the Third Ward's brewpubs.

Once we ordered dinner and drinks, she started in. "Are you in any stores yet?"

"I haven't opened up wholesale yet, as I'm not sure I want to be in stores," I explained. "I launched a wholesale channel in a previous job, and it was a lot of hand-holding. At this point, I prefer to sell direct-to-consumer."

"You need to be in stores," she replied. "No question. And you need to offer the insoles to the stores at $6 per pair."

What? You don't even know my costs. There's NO WAY I could do that.

She moved on without waiting for a response or noticing that my eyebrow had shot up in my confusion. "What do you have planned for product-line extensions?"

"I'm working on a couture version of the insole and a heel grip product with Insolia®," I replied. "I also have a formula for a foot spray that is designed to alleviate pain and reduce inflammation."

"Well, what you really need to do," she continued, "is make this insole in cork so that it wicks away moisture from the feet."

Huh? What is she talking about?

I was so confused by this conversation.

STEPPING ONTO THE STAGE

"And you should also sell them in butter boxes," she continued, "because apparently, these insoles help melt away the pain like butter."

Whoa, lady. Slow down.

Without taking a breath, she continued, "Where is your product housed?"

"It's currently warehoused at a fulfillment center just north of Minneapolis," I said.

"You need to move your inventory to Milwaukee. You need to see it and touch it every time a new shipment comes in."

Okay. That's valid.

The conversation went on like this for more than hour. At this point, all I wanted to do was go home and go to bed. It had been a long evening. I caught the eye of our waitress. "Check, please."

As I drove home, I thought about the fact that this lady had ideas. Plenty of ideas. But she fell into the 'cares more about my business than me' category. Though, she did have one good point.

I probably should move my inventory closer to Milwaukee—especially because I am developing new packaging and want to make sure it is put together correctly.

> Meri,
>
> You took an interest in my journey and found my story worthy of being told. While I wasn't at all polished, sharing my story publicly for the first time was an incredible experience. I miss seeing you every few weeks.
>
> *Amy Lou*

GETTING INTO THE GROOVE
YEAR 4 MONTH 4

Now that the weather was nice, I so badly wanted to be face up in the sun, but I spent the next several weeks head down, focusing on how to move Vivian Lou to the next level.

I sat at my desk in my red chair, and occasionally moved to the floor, pushing the cats and dog out of the way so I could lie in the warm sun.

Ahhh... there's nothing like a good dose of Vitamin D.

The first order of business was finding a new warehouse. So I Googled "Fulfillment centers in Milwaukee."

"MDS Fulfillment is a professional Midwest order fulfillment service company with creative fulfillment solutions and low shipping costs to grow your business."

Perfect!

"Hi, this is John," he answered when I called to inquire about fulfillment options.

"Hi, John. I'd love to chat with you about your services. I am the owner of Vivian Lou, a company that sells insoles for high heels..." I started.

After twenty minutes of conversation, he said, "Wow, Abby, this sounds like a great opportunity. I'm so sorry to turn you away, but you're not quite big enough yet. When you get a few more orders per day, we'd love to bring you on as a client."

Dang it!

I hung up the phone and went to the next option.

GETTING INTO THE GROOVE

"Hi, this is Lynn," she answered.

I once again introduced myself and Vivian Lou.

"We'd love to bring you on as a client," she said after ten minutes of chatting about my specific needs. "Yes, we can assemble the new packaging and handle both Shopify and Amazon order requests. Why don't you come in for a tour?"

Perfect! I will ask them to start assembling product and fulfilling orders once the new packaging is ready.

With a new fulfillment center selected, I transitioned my focus to the website, which needed to be updated to reflect my new packaging and new pricing.

UGH! Pricing. Why doesn't it still feel right?

I was committed to offering the insoles at $29 per pair as it was going to be in print in *O, The Oprah Magazine*™, but something still felt off.

What about the women who have multiple pairs of high heels? How do I empower her to wear all of her high heels 4x longer without pain . . . and without breaking the bank?

Later that afternoon while walking the dog, it hit me.

Bundles! Duh!

It was the perfect solution! I could offer two-pair, three-pair, four-pair, and five-pair bundles. Customers would receive one hardcover brochure and then bundled pairs in plastic bags.

The next day, I did the math and figured I could offer one pair for $29, two pairs for $39, three pairs for $49, four pairs for $59, and five pairs for $69.

Ooooooh . . . that's good.

The margin was doable, and the price breaks on multiple pairs would meet the needs of all customers. Heck, customers could now get the insoles for $13.80 a pair if they purchased a five-pair bundle. It was a great solution!

Okay, now that I have the pricing, it's time to address this website. Ugh.

I soaked up a few more rays on the floor and then got back to work.

NEW STEP

Up until now, I had done all of work on my website—all of it—and I was a bit hesitant to hand over the reins and spend the money. I had very limited HTML knowledge, but giving someone access to the backend of my store scared the bejesus out of me.

Once again sitting in my red chair, I used Shopify's expert search tool to find an expert designer in the area.

"Ethercycle in Chicago. An e-commerce consultancy helping Shopify stores grow their revenue."

Sign me up!

It was hard to wait the few days until Kurt—with Ethercycle—was available to chat, but I was glad when we connected.

"Hi, this is Kurt," he answered.

I introduced myself and Vivian Lou once again.

"I have an idea of what I'd like, but I need help getting it done," I confessed. I shared my ideas for bundles and color schemes and images and font types.

"No worries," he replied encouragingly. "We can definitely get this done for you."

Yes! Thank you!

Over the next few weeks, Kurt and his team diligently worked on the site, while I diligently asked annoying questions.

"Do you think I need a new website theme?" I prodded.

"The one you have is just fine, Abby," Kurt replied.

"Do you think the bundles make sense?" I asked.

"Yes, Abby, I think they make perfect sense," he confirmed. "We'll make it intuitive for people when they are on the product page."

"Do you think there's too much red?" I questioned.

"Nope. I think there's just the right amount," he answered patiently.

For some reason, I was nervous! Really nervous. It was easy to stress over the website when in reality, I was nervous about making it all work. The new packaging. The new price. And the new site. I had three months to make Vivian Lou profitable and time was ticking.

DING!

GETTING INTO THE GROOVE

It was an email from Tory Johnson Productions, inquiring about the possibility of featuring Vivian Lou Insolia® insoles on a special Oprah Edition of "View Your Deal," a popular segment featuring exclusive deals for viewers of *The View*. The show was scheduled to run on Monday, September 26, and Adam Glassman would present the insoles on the LIVE taping of the show.

Holy smokes! HOLY. SMOKES!

National exposure? Possibility of significant sales? New customer acquisition?

Yes! Yes! And yes! This is going to be life-changing. I just know it.

The following week, the kiddos were in camp for the day, Bill was at work, Edie and Papa, who were in town for their annual summer visit, were in the living room binge-watching Zoo on Netflix; and I was upstairs in my office when the doorbell rang.

"It's here!" I screamed as I raced downstairs to answer the door. I grabbed the FedEx package, ran into the kitchen, and tore open the envelope. "It's here!"

Pulver had finished printing my packaging and overnighted me a few samples.

Edie and Papa joined me in the kitchen as we looked over the samples.

"I love it!" I said hugging it to my chest. I held it out in front of me and stared at it. And then I nervously read the text.

Please Lord, let there be no typos.

I snapped some pictures and texted them to Bill and my family.

I love it!

In preparation for this day, Bill had picked up a bottle of something special—Dom Perignon.

Who knew you could buy Dom Perignon at Costco?

He hurried home that evening, and the four adults clinked glasses, while the kiddos sipped root beer.

"To new packaging. New websites. New pricing. And new opportunities."

Cheers to new beginnings! I knew this was the start of something amazing!

NEW STEP

I was so incredibly thankful and excited and nervous for all these new beginnings.

The only thing I don't really want to think about is HSN®. But I have to.

Sales on my online store totaled $3,000 in May, $2,500 in June, and I was on track to close July with $1,700 in online sales. HSN® was still my biggest sales channel.

Michael and I had spent quite a bit of time on the phone since his return from China, brainstorming ideas on how to create an insole for HSN® that I could sell as two-pair bundles for $19.95 and not compete with the $29 single pair and bundle options on my site.

"What about gold speckles?" he suggested one afternoon.

"What?" I asked intrigued.

"When we sold the product in Asia, we manufactured some insoles with gold speckles in the resin," he explained. "We could absolutely do that again. The insole wouldn't exactly be invisible though."

I loved the idea!

"That's okay," I confirmed excitedly. "It needs to be different!" Another idea suddenly came to mind, and I continued, "Could we also remove the contour lines on the surface of the insole so there's slightly less weight-shifting benefit?"

"I don't see why not," he said.

He confirmed the specifics with the factory, and I scheduled a call with HSN®.

"Michael, they agreed!" I exclaimed after speaking with the buying team a few days later. "We will name it Vivian Lou Insolia® Shimmer, and it will be an HSN®-exclusive insole."

"Congratulations, Abby," he said excitedly. "I'm so glad this worked out."

I was so happy and relieved that we had come to a resolution. HSN® still had quite a bit of inventory, so they weren't going to place any new orders until October, but this was definitely a step in the right direction.

Whew!

GETTING INTO THE GROOVE

Michael,

You listened to my rants, were the voice of reason, and found a solution. You still look out for my best interests, provide honest feedback, and make me feel like a part of the Insolia®/HBN® team. You are one of my biggest supporters, and I'm so grateful for this opportunity and your guidance.

Arry Lou

COURAGEOSITY
YEAR 4 MONTH 4

"Sales are still really slow," I admitted to Ursula during our twice-a-month sales coaching call. I felt embarrassed, and I could feel my cheeks getting hot as I said the words.

Ugh . . . I know I'm on the brink of something amazing, but how long is this going to take?!

I only had a month, maybe two if I were lucky, before Bill would no longer be okay with my not contributing to our current expenses and future investments.

I sat at my desk, staring at a paper that hung on the bulletin board on the wall opposite my chair. The paper was visible just beyond the view of my laptop screen, and it read, "Keep moving."

"You're on the right track, Abby," Ursula said reassuringly. "Your confidence will come."

Confidence.

I never liked the word confidence. I also don't like grit, hustle, grind, chops, drive, kill it, crush it, or smash it. These are in-your-face, aggressive, workout words.

And I don't like to work out.

I much prefer persistent, brave, resourceful, spirited, and tenacious. These are strong, powerful, yoga-like words.

And I like yoga.

It's a subtle difference, but building a business doesn't have to be a testosterone-fueled activity. You don't need to enter a market with a big bang. You can enter slowly, gracefully, and still be just as effective.

Ironically, my entrance was neither aggressive nor graceful. I stumbled, tripped, and rolled into this opportunity and into business. But here I was. Determined to make it work.

"You know what, Ursula? I'm okay if I'm never confident." I sat up a little straighter in my chair. "I see being confident as knowing all of the answers, believing that you know best, and having your shit together. And I am not any of these things," I smiled, thinking about how chaotic and unplanned this entire experience had been. "But I'm not afraid to jump, to ask for help, or to admit I have no idea what the hell I'm doing." I laughed at myself. "So I guess I'd rather be courageous and curious than confident." I paused and then said, "I'd rather have courageosity than confidence!"

"Abby," she replied in a very serious tone. "That's the subject of your book. Start keeping notes about your journey."

Oh Ursula, you're so funny! There you go again about the book!

But after our call ended, I opened up a blank document and spent the next hour bullet-pointing what had happened over the last few years.

Looking back, I cringed at the thought of working in a job that drained my soul and laughed at how excited I'd been about thirty-six readers for Mama's Shoes. I relived the manic moments volunteering for the Boulder startups and smiled at the thought of Darcy taking a chance on me. I chuckled at the foot spray attempts and then thought, *I will make that foot spray one day, damn it!*

I breathed a huge sigh of gratitude, remembering that first conversation with Brian when he detailed his struggle with selling the insoles and giggled at the thought of me wearing bright red heels to breakfast in Vegas.

Anything goes!

NEW STEP

I silently thanked Bill for empowering me to embark on yet another whim, and was overcome with gratitude for the folks that had been placed in my path since I started Vivian Lou.

I marveled at how much I had learned in such a short period of time. Yes, I was curious and courageous when it came to launching my business. But I was amazed at how curious and courageous I had been when it came to ME—coming face-to-face with and staring down my fears and self-limiting beliefs.

To courageosity!

O! THIS FEELS RIGHT
YEAR 4 MONTH 5

"Watch this, Mom!" Vivian yelled as she and William raced across the beach and belly flopped into Lake Michigan. The kiddos and I had just arrived in South Haven for our annual August trip, and we couldn't get to the water fast enough. After quickly unloading the car, we had thrown on our suits and headed across the street to meet my mom and dad for a day of fun in the sun.

The sun was high in the sky; its rays bounced off the rolling waves. And a gentle breeze blew under the beach umbrellas.

Today could not be more perfect!

DING!

I pulled out my phone to see a text from Ursula.

"Look what I just got in the mail!" Attached was a picture of the *O, The Oprah Magazine*™ cover and a picture of my $29 insoles in print.

OMG! This is amazing!

OMG! I am so excited!

OMG . . . my new site isn't LIVE yet!

It was August 4, and the site wasn't going to be LIVE until August 9.

"Hey Mom, can you keep an eye on the kiddos for a second? I have to make a quick call," I asked, squinting in her direction.

"Of course," my mom agreed, turning her gaze to the kids in the water.

I sprinted up to the house and called Kurt.

"Hey, any chance we can launch the site today?" I asked out of breath.

NEW STEP

"We're not ready with the code yet," he replied apologetically.

"No worries," I said calmly.

I don't know if it was the lake air or the soothing sun, but I wasn't panicked.

What's the worst thing that could happen? People go to my old site and purchase the insoles for a cheaper price than what's published in the magazine? No biggie!

I put away the phone and headed back to the beach to enjoy the amazing summer afternoon.

Over the next few days, Kurt and his team put the final touches on the updated website. On August 9, the new site went LIVE.

My heart was full. I was on the beach in South Haven, Michigan (my heaven on Earth) in August (my favorite month of the year), enjoying the warm sun (because Vitamin D), sitting with my sisters and my parents (love my family!), listening to my kiddos and their cousins squeal in delight (such an amazing sound) as they splashed in the lake (nothing better) when I saw it for the first time on my phone.

The new VivianLou.com site. Somebody pinch me!

Everything about Vivian Lou—the packaging, the pricing, and the website—FINALLY felt right.

It feels like ME.

I did a quick check of my numbers before putting my phone away for the day. I was now averaging five sales a day and was on track to close August with $3,700 in online sales. The business was not even close to being profitable yet, but somehow I knew it would be.

"It has to be," I whispered to myself as I tucked the phone away and shifted back into vacation mode.

O! THIS FEELS RIGHT

> Kurt,
>
> You have been and continue to be one of my most favorite partners. Your approach is simple. Your work is spectacular. And your knowledge of all things e-commerce is impressive. You don't have an agenda other than building profitable e-commerce sites. Thank you for bringing my vision and website to life.
>
> *ally lou*

RAPID ACCELERATION
YEAR 4 MONTH 6

"Do you want this nasty thing?" Amanda asked, pointing at a gold-framed replica of a 1911 Jules-Alexandre Grun painting. The artwork hung in her dining room as she was giving me a tour of their new home in Harland, Wisconsin.

"Are you serious?" I asked. "Why don't you want it?"

"It's hideous," she said with a scowl.

"YES!" I screamed. While I didn't particularly like the painting, I had been looking for a large, ornate, antique gold picture frame to hang behind my desk for quite some time.

I knew I wanted something to help me feel more grounded, more executive; and I had decided a few months ago that I wanted a large, gold ornate frame, but I hadn't found one I liked that was within my budget.

Until now.

I went home and immediately hung it up. With my large, ornate gold picture frame hanging behind me, I felt more committed to becoming visible in the world. I felt more in charge. I felt more worthy. I felt more courageous. And more committed to becoming visible in the world.

I had toyed with Facebook ads in the past, but didn't take it seriously and didn't have much success. I was on a new mission to figure it out. So I Googled "How to create Facebook ads."

Of course there were a million results. Some felt like bullshit. Others felt more legit. I learned what I could about the Facebook pixel, Power Editor tool, and ad best practices. And then I got to work.

RAPID ACCELERATION

I opened Canva and started creating my own ad graphics.

Hmmm . . . I'll try this image and the phrase "Wear high heels 4x longer without pain."

And then I'll try that image with the phrase "Finally! High heels without the hurt."

I launched small, like Darcy had taught me, and started testing some ads.

One ad in particular converted really well. (Mom: If you're reading this, a conversion happens when someone interacts with your ad and then takes a desired action. Sometimes that action is signing up for a newsletter or clicking to a specific webpage. In my case, the desired action was purchasing insoles on VivianLou.com.)

I spent $10 a day and was making around $40 a day in sales.

This is SO MUCH better than Google AdWords.

The reputable Google AdWords firm that I had hired a few months prior wasn't performing, and I had grown frustrated with their lack of results.

Maybe Google AdWords just won't work?

A week after seeing the success of my first Facebook ad, I called Darcy to get his opinion. "So I'm thinking about ending my relationship with the Google AdWords firm," I said. "I'm really bummed because I know they are really good and have worked well for you."

"Is anything working?" he asked.

"Well, I have this one Facebook ad that converts really well," I offered.

"How much are you spending on it a day?" he probed.

"Ten dollars," I replied proudly.

He laughed gently. "Why haven't you bumped up the budget to $100 a day?"

"I don't know," I replied, knowing full well why I hadn't increased the budget.

I had done the math. I closed August with $3,700 in online sales, and if I spent $100 a day in September, that would cost me $3,000. Since May, I had accumulated $29,000 worth of credit card debt due to the

NEW STEP

Google AdWords firm, website updates, inventory purchases, and new packaging. And I was nervous.

"Give it try," he encouraged.

"I should . . ." I agreed timidly.

"Let me know how it goes. Bye, Abby."

You have to do this, Abby. At this point, it's all or nothing. You have to go ALL IN.

I logged into Facebook and bumped the ad to $100 a day.*

(* I now know this is NOT the correct way to increase ad spend in Facebook. At the time, I had no idea.)

Later that day, the Google AdWords firm called to tell me they were dropping me as a client because I didn't meet their minimum monthly spend.

Oh, the irony!

• • •

A few days later, the family and I sat outside at Café Hollander after taking the kiddos on their first horseback-riding excursion at Appy Horse Acres in Fredonia, Wisconsin. It was a gorgeous September Sunday, and I was already two mimosas in and our food had not yet arrived.

"That's nuts, Abby," my dad laughed when I told him that I had been dropped by the Google AdWords firm the same day I increased my Facebook spend.

"It's only been a couple of days, but I am now averaging $800 a day in sales," I shared excitedly.

"Why haven't you bumped it up to $500 a day?" Bill chimed in with a smile.

Great question, Babe!

RAPID ACCELERATION

"I don't know," I replied excitedly and pulled out my cell phone. "Why don't I just do it right now?"

Boom!

I increased my ad spend to $500*.

(* Yes, jumping from $100 to $500 spend in a single day is nuts and not advised. Again, I had no clue.)

My mom sat across from me, eyes wide with awe. "You just did that on your phone?" she asked.

"Yep," I replied and took another sip.

"This is awesome!" my dad laughed.

Yeah, it's awesome all right, I thought as I took another gulp of my mimosa and put my phone away to enjoy the rest of the day.

. . .

HOLY SHIT!

"It's working! OMG! It's working! I made $2,300 in sales yesterday!" I screamed when I checked the store first thing the next morning.

This is freaking amazing!

I started checking my store every fifteen minutes and watched the numbers increase.

I can't believe this!

That week, I was averaging $3,100 a day in sales.

This is NUTS! This is happening so fast! Why haven't I focused on Facebook ads before now!?

I was selling the insoles so quickly that I placed an urgent (and huge!) purchase order with Insolia®.

As I sent the email off to Ken Schleicher at Insolia®, I smiled to myself, thinking, *One month ago, these numbers would have scared the shit out of me. Not today. Not anymore.*

NEW STEP

. . .

"Are you ready for tomorrow?" Gianna Fata of Tory Johnson Productions asked via email the morning of September 25.

I was so ready, but honestly had no idea what to expect.

OMG! Here we go!

The next morning, I fumbled with the remote to find the right channel on our TV, and found *The View* just in time to see Adam Glassman starting the "View Your Deal!" segment. I started videoing on my iPhone the moment he headed to the table with Vivian Lou Insolia® insoles.

"You wear high heels . . ." Adam said to show co-host and journalist Sara Haines, who followed behind him in her white dress and nude heels.

"I do wear high heels," she confirmed with a nod.

"And sometimes it's a little painful to wear high heels," Adam continued.

I was trembling with excitement as I watched and listened.

"Always painful," she agreed.

"Well," Adam said picking up an insole off the table. "This is going to change your high-heel wearing life. From Vivian Lou, this is an insole that prevents the cause of pain. So you can wear high heels 4x longer."

OMG! This is incredible! I can't believe what I'm seeing!

"So you can put these in any heel?" Sara asked, inspecting them closely with her eyes and fingertips.

"Any shoe," he confirmed. "Stock up on these, ladies! Put them in ALL of your shoes."

OMG! This is SO COOL!

As soon as the segment was over, I ran upstairs to my office and called my mom.

"Did you see it?!" I asked, out of breath.

"It was amazing!" Her excitement matched mine.

I quickly hung up with her and logged into the back end of the microsite we'd set up as part of "View Your Deal" to sell the insoles at 50 percent off for the next two days.

RAPID ACCELERATION

OH. MY. GOD.

In less than ten minutes, I had 100 orders.

There has to be a mistake.

But as I stared at the computer screen, the number continued to rise. Quickly. Very quickly.

How . . . can . . . this . . . be . . . ?

I was in complete and utter shock. I sat in my red office chair dumbfounded.

Holy shit. Is this really happening?

Riiiing. The Vivian Lou customer service line rang through to my cell phone.

Riiiing. Another call.

Riiing. Another.

What the hell?

I listened to the first voicemail.

"Hi. I saw your insoles on *The View* this morning, and I'm trying to purchase the bundles, but they appear to be sold out. Is this correct?"

Oh no!

I checked the next message.

"Hi. I'm trying to purchase the bundles on the 'View Your Deal' site, but they're sold out."

SHIT!

The bundles had sold out within fifteen minutes of the airing, and I scrambled to call the microsite developers.

"Remove the bundle options! Remove the bundle options!" I screamed as soon as I had them on the phone.

The bundles appeared on the microsite for less than five minutes after being sold out, but in that time, I received more than one hundred voicemails from customers who wanted to purchase them.

Holy shit.

Suddenly feeling faint, I laid down on my office floor, staring at the ceiling, unable to process what had just happened. It was only an hour

NEW STEP

after the show, and I had sold more insoles in that hour than I had sold in the past several months.

I stayed on the floor for probably twenty minutes, and then had to snap out of it.

There are more than one hundred voicemails to return!

"Abby, are you seeing these numbers?" my warehouse called later that afternoon. "This is amazing!"

It was amazing. Simply amazing.

DING DONG.

My doorbell rang, and I had to quickly finish the voicemail I was leaving for one of the customers who had called about the bundles.

"OMG, Abby!" my sister Rachel screamed as I opened the door. She handed me a little bottle of prosecco and a large silver balloon with brightly colored letters that read "BEST DAY EVER."

And it was pretty damn close to the best day ever.

Within forty-eight hours, I had sold more insoles via "View Your Deal" than I had sold through my online store since I launched the company almost two years ago.

Absolutely incredible.

I was able to pay off my credit card once again and had money to spare!

And just like that, I was operating from a different space. A new level of knowing. I had my Red Shoes. Because of "View Your Deal," Vivian Lou was now profitable. And thanks to Facebook ads, Vivian Lou would remain profitable. I wasn't going back to Corporate America.

I did it! Holy shit! I did it!

RAPID ACCELERATION

Adam,

You gave me your opinion when we first met at STORY, you featured Vivian Lou insoles in O, The Oprah Magazine™ and you flawlessly presented the insoles on "View Your Deal." These were such defining moments in my journey, and I am so grateful for your interest in these insoles. Thank you!

amy lou

Tory and Gianna,

This day was the turning point in my journey, and I am so incredibly thankful for you and your team.

amy lou

THINGS HAPPEN FOR A REASON
YEAR 4 MONTH 6

DING!

I looked down at my phone.

An email from Bill?

"Here are my thoughts on your presentation." And attached was a link to a Google Doc.

Presentation? What presentation?

I opened the link, and realized I was looking at his thoughts on the presentation I gave in June at Kit + Ace.

Why am I just getting this now? This email is dated June 22. That's odd.

It was 4:10 p.m. on September 27—the day after *The View*. I was slammed, trying to return the more than one hundred voicemails when I decided to take a breather to read his notes.

This is great feedback. I'll definitely take this into consideration for the next presentationnnnnn . . . HOLY SHIT!

I had completely forgotten.

I am presenting at 1 Million Cups—Milwaukee tomorrow morning. OMG! I haven't put together my presentation. I haven't picked out my outfit. And I have no idea where the meeting is being held.

I glanced at the clock. The kiddos were due home off the bus in twenty minutes, so I launched PowerPoint, started putting together my thoughts, and then headed downstairs to greet them at the door. Thank heavens Bill happily took over the night routine so I could prepare.

"Hi. Thank you so much for having me," I started the next morning.

I looked out at thirty faces, only two of which were female, and took a deep breath.

"I'd love to share with you what's happened to me in the last year . . ." and I simply told my story.

"Wow, Abby." One of the event organizers approached after I concluded my presentation. "You could tell that same story in front of a room of a thousand, and it would still be just as captivating. Good job!"

My story is captivating? Wow! I'm truly honored.

I stayed afterward to chat with folks who had gathered around to offer me the names of firms and individuals who may be able to help take Vivian Lou to the next level: a new Google AdWords agency, a tax advisor, and a CFO, to name a few.

Feeling incredibly grateful, I hopped in my car and sat for just a minute, reflecting on the past twenty-four hours.

I'd completely forgotten about this presentation when Bill's email arrived giving me just enough time to prepare so that I could come here to share my story again and receive a ton of fantastic referrals.

Chills ran up my arm.

The Universe really does have my back!

PARTNERS ON MY PATH
YEAR 4 MONTH 7

This is nuts! I thought to myself as I ran my hands through my hair in frustration, struggling to keep my spreadsheet of income and expenses in order.

Vivian Lou was now consistently making enough money that a spreadsheet would no longer do, and I was so bad at keeping records that I needed to enlist the support of a Chief Financial Officer—or at least someone who knew what the heck they were doing. Up to that point, I was lucky if I captured all of my expenses, and to be honest, my financials were a mess. I desperately needed help.

Oh wait!

I searched for an email I received from a gentleman I'd met at the 1 Million Cups—Milwaukee event. He highly recommended FinePoint Consulting, a firm out of Madison, Wisconsin, that helps startups and early stage companies with accounting and CFO advisory services.

Perfect!

I connected with their founder and decided to move forward with their services. A few days later, the agency's welcome email read, "We are so excited to welcome you aboard!"

You're not nearly as excited as I am!

I was relieved that FinePoint would get my books up to date and maintain them going forward.

Now for the fulfillment center!

Sitting forward in my red chair, I decided to take another big step.

PARTNERS ON MY PATH

I was having issues with my current fulfillment center. Sending the wrong sizes. Sending the incorrect number of pairs in bundles. Missing shipments. It was bad, and I was desperate to leave.

I found the number again and dialed.

"Hi, John," I started when he answered the phone at MDS Fulfillment just a short four months after our initial conversation. "It's Abby Walker with Vivian Lou. I think I'm big enough now," I said, smiling through the phone.

He laughed. "Why don't you come in for a tour, and we'll talk through what exactly you need from us."

Five days later, I toured their facility and waited for their proposed rates.

While I waited for their rates, I kept busy answering customer service emails and phone calls. The increased sales from Facebook ads brought an increase in customer service inquiries. After a few weeks of handling everything myself, I felt ragged and realized something had to change.

I'm overwhelmed. How will I continue to do this?

I knew I couldn't spend all of my time on the phone and answering customer inquiries—I had to free up time to focus on marketing, partnerships, and new products.

But I really don't want to let this go!

Customer service happened to be a hallmark of Vivian Lou. I prided myself on treating customers with respect, refunding purchases without asking questions, and accommodating unusual requests to make customers happy. I would need to make sure whomever was going to take over for me would do the same.

I had no idea where to begin, so I Googled: "Customer service virtual assistant."

Thousands of virtual assistant companies appeared, and I spent a good day researching several firms and then reached out to three firms via their "Contact Us" forms.

DING!

NEW STEP

From: Randi Brown
To: Abby Walker
Date: Wed, Oct 26 at 10:43 AM
Subject: Contemporary Virtual Assistance

Hi Abby!

This is Randi, from Contemporary VA. I received your request that you would like information about Contemporary VA and how we can assist you with customer service. I'd love to set up a time for us to connect to discuss how we could assist you! You can schedule a time that is convenient for you at https://xxxx.com (all times are Eastern Time). If you do not see a time that will work with your schedule, please let me know and I will work to accommodate you.

Thank you and I look forward to speaking with you soon!!

That was quick!

I set up time with Randi and explained that I needed a virtual assistant to handle customer service, but that I was extremely nervous about letting go of this critical customer touchpoint.

"I know it is asking a lot, but I want someone with the same approach, the same demeanor, and the same writing style."

"I completely understand, Abby," she consoled me. "I have just the person for you."

From: Christina McCandlish
To: Abby Walker
Date: Fri, Oct 28 at 1:04 PM
Subject: Re: VA Introduction

Hi Abby!

It's a pleasure to "meet" you! I'm excited about your business and the great strides you've made in marketing and promoting your product (which I LOVE!).

PARTNERS ON MY PATH

As Bethany mentioned, I've worked with CVA as the lead Client Advocate managing our sales, marketing and customer service teams here prior to transitioning into a VA role. Customer service, social media and marketing are my specialties and I look forward to helping you with these needs moving forward!

Please, feel free to review my calendar here: https://xxxx.com for a time we can connect to get acquainted and I'll look forward to talking then. Until then, please, don't hesitate to share any log in's, company details or projects you'd like me to review or get started on.

I will be out of the office on Monday morning, but reachable by email. My mother is having surgery, and I'm needed at the hospital. I do appreciate your understanding, and look forward to getting to know you!

Warmest Regards,
Christina

I nearly jumped out of my red chair when I saw it.

OMG! She started her email the way I start all of my emails. She used exclamation points where I would have used them! She used all caps when writing 'LOVE'! I LOVE this lady!

I was so excited and relieved, I could hardly contain myself!

I immediately purchased a pool of hours from the firm and asked that Christina handle my customer service.

In preparation for the hand off, I put together templates of how I typically responded to certain inquiries. And off we went. The moment Christina had access to the customer service email box, she took over and nailed it.

Dang! This lady is GOOD!

I started checking the customer service email box a little less frequently and once again had the time to think and act big. I started testing more ads, brainstormed product line extensions, and pursued partnerships with storefronts like Fancy.com and Gilt.com.

It felt good to be proactive again!

NEW STEP

I'd had an amazing few months, and I knew that I was setting myself up to sustain the growth.

> Christina,
>
> It was so very hard for me to let go of this critical piece, but you picked it up flawlessly and, from Day One, have represented Vivian Lou far better than I ever did. Having you handle customer service has been life-changing. Thank you for allowing me the space to focus on new ideas and the future of Vivian Lou.
>
> *Amy Lou*

ONE GIGANTIC STEP
YEAR 4 MONTH 8

It was the day before Thanksgiving, and it was a pretty typical day. The kiddos went to school. Bill headed to work. And I walked upstairs to my office with a warm cup of coffee in hand.

I had purchased a Keurig at Costco as a celebratory gift to myself after *The View* and was now drinking Caribou's morning blend.

As I sat down at my desk and looked out the window, I was overcome with emotion.

I have so much to be thankful for!

I closed October with $110,000 in online sales and was slated to close November with $120,000 in online sales. HSN® placed their first purchase order for Vivian Lou Insolia® Shimmer insoles, and I had plenty of cash in the bank. I no longer carried a credit card balance and was able to pay off all expenses at the end of every month.

This was also the day that MDS started fulfilling orders, and I would start sleeping better at night, knowing that orders were going to be filled and shipped correctly.

Edie, Papa, and my brother-in-law, Scott, were headed into town; and the next day, we were celebrating the holiday with my side of the family at Amanda's house.

I did it. I escaped the good life. I found my Red Shoes.

I blinked away tears of gratitude, took a deep breath, and focused on tying up all of the loose ends before the holiday weekend.

NEW STEP

When I finished all of the usual daily activities, I trembled as I started a new task. It was one I had never attempted before, and I was beyond excited about the impact it was going to have.

. . .

After the kiddos had gone to bed and our out-of-town guests were watching a movie in the living room, I found Bill in the kitchen.

"Here you go, Honey," I said, handing him a folded piece of paper.

"What's this?" he asked, reaching out to take it from me.

He curiously unfolded the paper, paused, and looked up at me with a huge smile.

It was a check made out to Abigail Walker in the exact amount of my monthly corporate salary.

I was now a full-blown entrepreneur that could pay herself enough to cover her lost monthly salary . . . and then some.

"Congratulations, Honey," he said as he pulled me in for a hug. "I am so proud of you."

We stood in an embrace in the middle of the kitchen, not saying anything—just breathing sighs of relief.

This was a big day for me. This was a big day for him. This was a big day for us.

He squeezed me tight, kissed me on the top of the head, and headed back into the living room to finish the movie with his family. As he walked away, I noticed his shoes. His red suede Puma trainers.

Of course! I giggled to myself. *Now it's his turn.*

ONE GIGANTIC STEP

Bill,

    Holy smokes, Babe! I honestly didn't realize how difficult this journey must have been on you until I wrote this book. Thank you for being my partner, my protector, my cheerleader, my launchpad, and my safety net. Thank you, thank you, thank you for not saying NO. Thank you for giving me the freedom, the space, and the time to pursue my random impulses. Thank you for reining me in when I stepped outside the boundaries of our agreement. Thank you for masterfully negotiating our arrangements and for never once questioning my ability to achieve this dream. Thank you for picking up the kiddos, making dinner, and doing bath time when I needed you to cover for me. I thought I was the kinder, more patient, more understanding person in our relationship; and I proved myself wrong time and time again in telling this story! Ha ha ha! I am a far different person today than the day we got married. Thank you for sticking by my side and evolving with me. I am truly the luckiest girl in the world and am so incredibly excited and honored to support you in your journey for something more. I promise to be your partner, protector, cheerleader, launchpad, and safety net. Just don't expect me to do the laundry! Here's to your Red Shoes, Babe! May your journey include loads of new tools, a pickup truck, and not too many broken toilets! I love you THIS MUCH!

Ary Lou

TIPS FOR YOUR QUEST

Dear Reader,

Thank you for allowing me to share my journey! When I first decided to write this book, I struggled with whether it was "selfish" to tell my story. But thanks to my amazing message and book coach, Amanda Johnson, my fellow writing retreaters, Torey and Mary, and of course, Greg, that limiting belief quickly disappeared.

If you dream about something different. If you yearn for more freedom. If you long to believe in yourself. If you are ready to jump. I hope that my story somehow inspires you to take the first step or the next step—however small it might be. You don't need to know what your end will look like in order to start. You will figure it out along the way.

When you are ready to begin your Red Shoe journey, here are just a few tips that helped me along the way and may help you as well.

Be curious.

Everyone starts at the same spot—with just an idea. Or in my case, just a question. I encourage you to see where your idea or question leads you. Be open to endless possibilities. Ask yourself, "Why not me?" Give in (just a little) to that burning desire inside of you.

Trust your gut.

Some call it intuition. I call it a gut reaction. Whatever you want to call it, it's a powerful tool. I've not yet been steered in the wrong direction by my gut. Sometimes it is an instant reaction to something or someone. Other times, it takes time to assess a situation, but I always know which way to go. Trusting your gut takes practice, but it's like a muscle—the more you use it, the stronger it becomes.

Change your underwear.

Ha! Yes. For years, I only purchased black underwear. Perhaps I was mourning the good life? But one day, I purchased colored underwear (in full disclosure, I purchased the colored undies because they were the only ones on sale)! But I soon discovered that brightly colored underwear is inspiring! If I had a lot to accomplish or needed to make a big decision, I would wear my bright red or fuchsia undies, and somehow they made me feel more empowered, more inspired, more courageous. Perhaps they were the needed fire under my butt?! What a difference! I've since updated my drawer to include much more colorful options.

Be comfortable being uncomfortable.

It's hard at first, but eventually you will get used to it. Push or throw yourself outside of your comfort zone. Do things you once thought impossible. Take just one risk.

Post sticky notes.

I have sticky notes with the word "YES!" written on them posted everywhere in my office. On my bookshelf, on my computer, on a window, on the door. These notes have been placed around my office for so long that I no longer see them, but by having them there, I'm surrounded by "YES!" energy and subconsciously remind myself that 'YES!' I can do this.

NEW STEP

Don't compare your beginning to someone else's middle.

This was one of the hardest lessons learned for me, as I constantly compared myself to others. As soon as I determined that this was my unique journey, things instantly became more fun and flowed more easily. It's your journey. Keep your eyes on the road and stay in your lane. You will reach your destination.

Dance it out.

If you're stuck or uninspired or down, turn on some music—whatever kind of music makes you move. Turn it up and dance. Jump. Shake it out. Look at yourself in the mirror. Watch yourself loosen up and have fun.

Devour free content.

There is so much free content available. You don't need to spend unnecessary money (or money you don't even have) on courses or "how-tos"—at least when you're first starting out. Figure out exactly where you need the most help and Google it. Often, free content is just as good as paid content. If and when you decide to invest in a course or a program, make sure it meets your exact needs before enrolling.

Buck the system every once in a while.

I love listening to the latest advice on subjects from website design to Facebook ads. And I tend to do the opposite of what the latest gurus have to say. I've had extreme success not listening to "conventional wisdom." When everyone said to niche Facebook ads, I did the opposite and advertised to everyone. It worked. When folks said that I shouldn't offer free shipping, I put a banner at the top of my website advertising my free shipping. It worked. Do what feels right to you . . . even if that means doing it your own way.

Don't call it a hobby.

Whatever your journey or quest, don't call it a hobby. If you do, the Universe will treat it as a hobby. Call it a dream. Call it a mission. Call it a calling. Don't be embarrassed or timid or shy. State your desires out loud or just to yourself in your head. But state them so that the Universe can hear them and know you're serious.

Swear.

Okay, I understand swearing isn't for everyone. But occasionally it feels damn good, and sometimes it's fucking necessary. I subscribe to the theory that those who swear a lot are more honest and trustworthy. People often ask if I swear in front of the kiddos, and the answer is YES. I'm not proud of it, but I'm also not ashamed of it. Bill and I have our master's degrees, so we tell the kiddos that once they earn their master's degree, they can swear. And it's worked thus far! We'll see how long we can get away with it. In full disclosure, our approach is borrowed from my dad, who used to say that swear words were "legal terms." And once we received our JD, we could swear.

Seek help if needed.

I knew I had issues feeling worthy . . . and it became increasingly evident that I also had issues with money. I found help with Greg and Ursula. If you feel resistance to success, I encourage you to seek help. You may be able to release your self-limiting beliefs simply by recognizing them and choosing to ignore them. You may be able to release them by talking it through with a friend. Or if you're like me, you will need to invest in professional assistance! Either way, know you are not alone! Turns out, not feeling worthy and having issues or resistance to money are common blocks.

NEW STEP

Focus.

Being an entrepreneur, you can quickly get overwhelmed by how much there is to do. It helped me to focus on one task at a time. Decide on the task. Finish it. Cross it off your list. And then move on to the next. The more you cross off, the more inspired you become to keep going. Launching a business takes a lot of work, but it's not all hard. It just takes focus. And remember, you don't have to hustle or grind your way through it. Work at an intensity and pace that's comfortable for you.

Fail quickly.

You're going to fail. Somewhere along your journey, you will fail. Everyone does. Your prototype breaks. Your ad doesn't convert. Your partnership falls apart. You have a typo on your packaging. Whether big or small, you're going to fail. And it's okay. The sooner you become comfortable with failing, the quicker you will recover. And there is nothing more empowering than admitting a failure, learning a lesson, and applying that lesson to your next action.

Start a "Read This When You Get Insecure" file.

Fill this file with quotes, inspirational stories of other entrepreneurs, links to videos, profiles of people you admire—anything that gets you motivated and inspired. When you're having a bad day, open it up and reignite the fire.

Keep moving.

There will be days when you will want to throw in the towel. Keep moving. There will be days when you've surpassed all expectations. Keep moving. There will be days when you have no sales. Keep moving. There will be days with tremendous sales. Keep moving. Whatever you're feeling—recognize it, accept it, and then keep moving. It's all part of the journey. The key is to keep moving and stay the course.

Create your own highlight reel.

Regardless of how big or seemingly little your wins are, celebrate them! Write them down, do a little shimmy, and then high-five your dog. You don't need to shout your big or small wins from the rooftops, but you can and need to recognize your work and your accomplishments. And speaking of highlight reels, be sure to keep notes on your journey. One day, you will look back and giggle at how far you've come.

Choose your dream. And then choose it again.

One of my favorite quotes is from Ursula Mentjes' book *One Great Goal*. In it, she writes, "If a dream has been placed on your heart and is circulating through your mind, THAT IS YOUR MESSAGE! The message cannot be any clearer. Stop questioning what you already know." Later, she writes, "Choose [that dream]. And then choose it over and over again." Listen to the little whispers. Follow that burning desire. Identify your dream. And once you do, choose that dream again and again.

Don't stop until you find those Red Shoes.

Launching and growing Vivian Lou has been a wild adventure; but perhaps the greater story is my personal journey. Beyoncé once said, "I don't like to gamble, but if there's one thing I'm willing to bet on, it's myself." When I first read this quote, I was in awe. I wanted to believe in myself the way she believed in herself. I so badly wanted to feel that—live that. It took some courage, some curiosity and a lot of work on ME, but I'm happy to say that today, I believe in myself more than I ever have and it is an unbelievable gift. Don't stop until you find yourself. The journey,

NEW STEP

the tears, the late nights, the pushing yourself to get comfortable with the uncomfortable will all be worth it!

My wish for you is that that you find the curiosity to try something new, pick up the phone, or Google something you don't know . . . and the courage to choose your dream again and again, admit your weaknesses, or launch before you're ready—so that your dreams become your reality.

To courageosity and finding your Red Shoes!

Amy Lou

ACKNOWLEDGMENTS

To Bill, thank you for saying, "No." And then *not* saying, "No." And then saying, "Yes, but . . ." Thank you for tolerating my whims, for giving me time, for never questioning my ability to achieve this dream. Thank you for being an amazing father to our children, for being a patient husband, for being our unwavering protector, and for knowing how to put together a blender. I am so incredibly thankful for you! I honestly don't know how you put up with me! I love you more than words!

To my kiddos, thank you for your love and your patience. I am so incredibly proud of you and honored to be your mom!

To my mom and dad, thank you for your encouragement and your honest feedback! And Mom, thank you for allowing me to "use" you to explain certain terms throughout this book. I'm sorry if I make you look uninformed.

To Ursula, thank you for your vision, your insight, your knowing—for gently pushing me outside of my comfort zone, and for "holding" this book for me until I was ready to hold it for myself. Oh, and for suggesting I keep notes.

To Greg, thank you for your empathy and your understanding, for helping me uncover and obliterate (ha!) my issues, and for guiding me to peace.

To Amanda Johnson, thank you for your guidance, your time, your humor, your interest, your expertise, and your confidence. The book—in this form—would not have happened without you!

To the amazing cast of characters who have helped me in my quest for the Red Shoes, thank you! Thank you! Thank you!

ABOUT ABBY LOU

Abby Lou Walker is the CEO of Vivian Lou Inc., a company with multi-million dollar annual sales dedicated to helping women look and feel better in high heels. She started her company as a "hobby" business (while being a full-time working mom) after picking up the phone and asking one simple question.

This "hobby" made her feel alive again. She had finally found something that quieted her burning desire for something more; and a short two years later, she strapped on a pair of her favorite high heels and walked away from Corporate America.

Her mission as the CEO of Vivian Lou is to empower women to wear heels four times longer without pain so they can focus more on their dreams and less on their feet.

She's written *New Step* to inspire those who are meant for more to take the first step—or the next step—toward finding their something more.

Prior to starting her own company, Abby served as Chief Marketing Officer for a natural supplements company; Vice President of Account Management and Communications for a financial services company; and Senior Director, Internal Communications at a large financial planning company. She received her master's degree in Business Communication

ABOUT ABBY LOU

from DePaul University, Chicago, Illinois, and her bachelor's degree in English-Journalism from Miami University, Oxford, Ohio.

Abby currently resides in Colorado with her amazing husband and is Mom to two incredible kiddos, a couple of cats, and a loveable old dog.

She loves the color red, bubbly beverages, and all things chocolate. She laughs a bit too loud and uses words like Awesome, Amazing, and Great. She craves long hugs from good friends, the smell of fresh-cut grass, and heart-printed pajama pants.

She believes in helping those less fortunate, in encouraging others to accomplish their dreams, and in women promoting and supporting other women. She cheers for women who have found their niche, hit their stride, and silenced self-doubt.

She makes pancakes for dinner, loves South Haven, Michigan, and believes that a great pair of shoes can change your perspective on everything.